GOOD WINE BAD LANGUAGE GREAT VINEYARDS

WINE CHARACTERS OF NEW ZEALAND

photographed by esmeralda wood

For
Leela Lakshmi Murdoch Badami

contents

foreword

Hey, call me a winery junkie, a terroir terrorist, or just drunk on the love of it, but to me, it's all the same: how much I've come to passionately enjoy wine and become infected by the passion and joy of those who make it.

Whether you're a good-time slurper or a fine-dining "sip-swish-and-spitter", you'd agree that it's about time we took a good look at the influence New Zealand wines are starting to have all over the world, winning awards and selling in ever increasing volumes everywhere from London to New York… to Sydney. And beyond!

So, after the Aussies had their turn and after all the fun we had introducing you to some of Australia's great Australian Wine Characters in Good Wine, Bad Language, Great Vineyards, the first edition. I'm especially proud to bring you thirty-four of Aotearoa's most interesting and accomplished Wine Characters.

Like most wine novices, I'd always believed that wineries were serious, mysterious places, involving dark, arcane secrets which mere mortals could never understand - let alone appreciate. Growing up in New Zealand in the 80s, where everybody guzzled DB beer, wine seemed something toffs drank in expensive old clubs somewhere far away… but things have cetainly changed now.

Pretentious "wine speak" aside, once you've gone on a journey through the vineyards and lives of these amazing people, you'll be astounded by their energy, their enthusiasm, charming perspective - and their good humour! It's like this…Juicy little grapes + (passion x vision) + hard work ÷ (planting + pruning + picking + pressing) + (more hard work x 2) + (bottling x cellaring) = something so simple and special - a good bottle of wine.

And if it's a great bottle of wine, enjoyed round the table with good food and friends' laughter, guess who gets all the credit? Yes, you, you clever thing! What great taste you have!

And yet, for all that magic, once you cut through the "quaff", you'll discover how down-to-earth these unsung heroes in the wine industry are. Not that they flaunt their viticultural qualifications or oenological expertise, they just focus on the most important thing of all - the best wine for people to enjoy. You'll meet cheesemakers and furniture makers; yachtsmen and racing car drivers; families and young couples; a punk and a direct descendant of the Black Prince. All sorts - and all good sorts too.

Esmeralda's once again illustrated this fantastic voyage with some of her best photos, capturing not just the stunning landscape of New Zealand's wine regions, but the characters who live and work in them.

Sunil, who's worked with me on many of my previous books, returned from the UK with his lovely wife April in time for this book. And, in the middle of everything, to have their beautiful daughter Leela Lakshmi, to whom this book's dedicated with much love.

We crammed in all 26 wineries in just sixteen days, and though we greatly enjoyed the chance to meet and hang out with everyone, we'd love to go back with much more time up our sleeves. But you don't have to rush! You can enjoy the journey from the comfort of your favourite chair. Just curl up with a glass of something yum, sit back, relax, and map out who you'll drink next… because, remember, wine is good times bottled.

Cheers!
Hayden Wood, aka 'Woody'
AUTHOR OF THE LIQUID KITCHEN

coopers creek wines

coopers creek wines

simon nunns - chief winemaker

Having spent a "wonderful weekend in Hawke's Bay and Gisborne, sampling the wines", Coopers Creek's winemaker Simon Nunns decided to quit his IT job and become a winemaker. He ended up graduating with distinction in Viticulture and Oenology from Lincoln University in 1995 and travelling the world, working on vintages in Oregon, Burgundy and Bordeaux. His first vintage was actually at Coopers Creek as a cellar-hand in 1993, before returning in 1997 as assistant winemaker under the renowned Kim Crawford, before becoming Chief Winemaker in 1998.

Just as Coopers Creek prides itself on growing a wide range of new and interesting grape varieties, including Arneis, Viognier and eleven others, Simon has an eclectic range of interests, including medieval history and designing his own furniture. Oh, and a female Italian Greyhound called Guido ("because we'd decided on the name before we got the dog," Simon says. As you do) and a hairless Sphynx cat called Edmund (after Blackadder, of course)…

What do you love best about what you do?
I guess the main thing's creating something that brings enjoyment not just to me but also to others. And also because no two vintages are the same, especially as we've got so many different grape varieties at Coopers Creek - we have about thirteen on the go at the moment.

Are you competitive with your partner, who's also a winemaker?
Well, Katrina's the Auckland winemaker for Nobilo, which is part of the Constellation Group (the same company as Hardy's)… but no, I don't think we really are (laughs) - we just cruise along.

What are your favourite grape varieties and why - white and red?
We've always got new varieties coming up. There's a lot of new and exciting stuff happening now, and what's really exciting me at the moment is Viognier, just because it's such an exotic variety and the flavour's so fabulous; and Arneis (which rhymes with "place"), from the Italian Piedmont because despite being so difficult to grow and make into wine, it's so new and we're one of only two producers of it at the moment so we're right on the cutting edge of things there; and on the red front, the grape that's really getting me excited at the moment is Syrah, again because it's relatively new for us and it's a variety with a lot of potential

And in a few years, it'll be Alborino from North West Spain and Northern Portugal as it makes very aromatic wines, not too dissimilar to Sauvignon Blanc. So it's always extremely exciting to be a winemaker here!

What's your favourite hangover cure?
I reckon you should hit it with everything - Disprin, Berocca, something fatty, something sweet, strong coffee… and a ginger beer (I like pork belly and a bag of Pascal's Party Mix)!

What's your favourite drinking game?
We used to play a game called "Whiz" at uni, involving hand signals and vocalisations - although the rules'd be too complicated to explain… or quite remember - though you'd get it soon enough if you saw it in action!

What's the best glass of wine you've had?
Probably a glass of 1983 Chateau d'Yquem - it was a stunning wine, but it was also part of a stunning line up of wines at a great dinner we had once, which included a 1951 Burgundy, 1962 Chateau Margaux, a couple of 74 California Cabernets, and a 77 Taylor's Port.

Have you ever drunk cask wine?
Yes, definitely - I was a student once!

simon nunns

What do you do to relax?
I've got a bit of a lawn mowing fetish - I love mowing the lawns. I think it's driven out of my desire to create a little order out of disorder. And I design my own furniture.

Is designing furniture similar or different to winemaking?
It's similar - you've got to be both artistic and practical. I guess it's not quite as involved as winemaking, because I'm doing it in a pretty simplistic fashion.

What music do you listen to at work?
Generally you've got to move to a pace at work, especially at vintage, so it tends to be stuff with a bit of energy to it like electronica or reggae, but nothing commercial! If you heard it on the radio, you're unlikely to hear it on the cellar stereo.

Who would you most like to share a glass of wine with?
They called him "the Nose" - a Spanish guy called Ignacio Domecq - he was supposed to have an almost superhuman sense of smell and tasting ability… because I like sherry and he could tell me all about it - he was the winemaker for the famous wine company called Domecq.

wine
Coopers Creek's philosophy is to grow grape varietals in the regions they perform best, as well as innovating with unusual or new varieties such as Arneis and Alborino.

Its premium Select Vineyards range includes "The Little Rascal" Gisborne Arneis and "Chalk Ridge" Hawke's Bay Viognier, both of which come from selected single vineyards - hence the name! The Little Rascal's an Arneis grown in its Gisborne vineyard. The Arneis grape is native to Piedmont in North West Italy, and its name means "Little Rascal", reflecting in two words just how difficult this wine is to grow and vinify (winespeak for "turn into wine"). Although young, it's surprisingly rich, with stone-fruit touches and delicate herbal characters. Some of the guys in the cellar thought they could detect hints of almond, which is typical of Arneis. If it behaves the way it does in Italy, it won't be a wine for the cellar - but there's not much of it, so buy it and drink it, Simon says, especially with seafood and salads.

"Chalk Ridge" is the second prize-winning Viognier vintage from the new Chalk Ridge block in Hawke's Bay. It's so called because of the fractured, chalky limestone soil, on a steep block that's difficult to work, but which produces a big, rich wine with flavours of peach

and apricot blossom. It's a great match to chicken and fish and like most Viogniers, doesn't require long cellaring - it's best enjoyed young.

The Swamp Reserve Chardonnay's legendary, having garnered a trove of awards, being ranked New Zealand's second-highest rated Chardonnay by the prestigious Cuisine Magazine and awarded 97/100 points by Australian Gourmet Traveller Wine Magazine. It exhibits ripe citrus characters with great harmony and balance, which is reflected in this complex, full-bodied wine, whose sweet fruit flavours go brilliantly with rich meat, poultry and seafood dishes. Whatever you have it with, why not try it with citrus, apple or mushroom sauces, well-seasoned with aromatic herbs?

vineyard

Founded in 1980 by Andrew and Cynthia Hendry, and only 30 minutes' drive from the heart of Auckland, Coopers Creek sources its grapes from both its own vineyards and from specialist growers, believing in using only the best varietals and growing them in places they'll grow best, such as the Gimblett Gravels in Hawke's Bay, an old river bed with very stony soil, where Merlot, Cabernet Sauvignon and Cabernet Franc are grown.

A comprehensive range of current and older vintage wines are always available for tasting at the cellar door. In addition to enjoying purchases in Coopers Creek's idyllic, sculpture adorned gardens, you can also find petanque (or French "boules") courts, a full-size outdoor chess board and great children's playground. And feel free to enjoy the complimentary barbecue facilities when you bring your own picnic lunch, whether during the live jazz concerts held every Sunday in summer, or the planned weekend farmers' market.

Coopers Creek Winery
601 State Highway 16 Huapai (just north of Kumeu)
ph [64 9] 412 8560
info@cooperscreek.co.nz   www.cooperscreek.co.nz
Cellar Door: Open 9.30am - 5.30pm Monday to Friday and 10.30am - 5.30pm Weekends & Public Holidays
Online ordering is available for New Zealand residents.

mills reef

mills reef

tim preston - winemaker

Inspired by his father Paddy's life-long passion for winemaking, Tim Preston followed in his footsteps and became an award-winning winemaker himself, co-founding Mills Reef with his father in 1989. It didn't take long for their winery to become one of New Zealand's most lauded - and for them to become one of its most celebrated winemaking teams.

"Dad's passion for winemaking - and life - passed over to me, right from day one out of school," says Paddy's affable and modest son, Tim. "Starting winemaking with Dad was awesome and it was great bonding: we started together, and though we've faced many challenges over the years, we got through them and we're much stronger for it." Paddy - real name Warren Mills Preston - still takes an active role in the winery, working with Tim to hand-craft superb wine, allowing Tim, with his "youthful" exuberance, to take a travelling ambassadorial role in promoting their wine and winery.

The family's original idea for their winery was to have a name that wasn't only unique but had meaning and told a story. And what a story! Mills Reef refers to Paddy's great grandfather Charles Mills, a sea captain who was also involved in mining, eventually becoming Minister for Trade and Customs in the early 1900s. You could say Mills Reef refers to both coral and gold reefs! Tim can't say for sure whether his illustrious ancestor ever found his "reef" but he knows for sure he and his family have found theirs in following their own passions and making wine they're truly proud of…

How did you and your dad get into winemaking?
Dad did all sorts of things, including butchery and building, before the opportunity arose to become a winemaker. He'd always made wine at home when I was a kid, but when he was about 45 or 50, and I'd just come out of school, he went with his passion and took me along for the ride!

What's it like working with your Dad?
Well, there's huge highs but it's a very honest relationship - we've been doing it for 20-odd years now, so I guess we're used to each other now!

What's the worst wine "faux pas" you've ever made?
I have a very short memory on that sort of thing!

What do you drink apart from wine?
If I drink too much beer I swell up like the Michelin Man! I'm a wine man through and through.

What do you do to relax?
Mainly blokey pursuits like golf, fishing and hunting deer.

Any good venison recipes?
Cook it with anchovy butter! Our big reds, like the Bordeaux varieties or the Elspeth Syrah go very well with it.

What's your favourite grape varieties and why - white and red?
Chardonnay and Syrah and probably both for the same reason. It's what you can do and create as a winemaker and the influence you can have on those two varieties that reflects your distinct style.

What's your favourite drinking game?
If you talked to the guys in the cellar, it'd have to be Jacks, which is a silly card game where you drink when your card comes out of the pack. Basically, cards are dealt out round the table and the guy with the first Jack chooses the drink; the guy with the

tim preston

second Jack says how much you have to drink; and the guy with the third has to drink it. I don't tend to do very well at it!

What's your party trick?
It involves a coin and funnel. You put the funnel at the top of someone's pants, and the coin goes on their forehead when their head's tilted back. Then they have to put the coin in the funnel three times to get $100. But if they get the coin in twice, you pour a glass of cold wine down the funnel!

What's the strangest job you've ever had apart from winemaking?
When we first started winemaking, before the first vintage came off, we had ten acres of young pine trees. My job was turning those trees into fence posts which was bloody hard yakka - luckily it only lasted a year!

Who's your favourite cartoon or superhero?
I'd have to say Sponge Bob Square Pants because my kids got me on stage at a fun park with him and I got a cream sponge in my face!

What's your favourite wine region outside yours?
It'd have to be Alsace. I'm sure that's because of the experience I had there with a very old family winery that'd been handed down through generations. Everything about it - the history, the traditions, the landscape - was breathtaking.

What would your last meal be - and what wine would go with it?
It would have to be the seafood with caviar and salmon along with Krug champagne, my absolute favourite!

wine

When Paddy and Tim first purchased the Mere Road Vineyard in 1992, it was planted with typical Marlborough aromatic varietals: Chardonnay, Sauvignon Blanc, Chenin Blanc and Pinot. Knowing it was in a very special part of Hawke's Bay, they took the plunge and replanted the whole place with traditional Bordeaux varieties and Syrah. When the first harvest came off, Paddy was convinced these were special wines, and so gave them the premium label "Elspeth" in honour of Paddy's own mum, a gracious lady who enjoyed and lived life to the fullest: a philosophy very much reflected in the personality, style and quality of Elspeth wines, which are only produced when Tim and Paddy feel the vintage and fruit are of exceptional enough quality, something proven by their astounding track record, having won over 500 Gold Medals and 14 trophies over the years, and being named NZ Winemaker of the Year two years' running!

Handcrafted from vine to wine, Mills Reef's Elspeth One is so called because of the unique union of five varieties - merlot, cabernet sauvignon, cabernet.franc, Malbec and Syrah - into one truly triumphant wine, which thanks to one of the best vintages in the Gimblett Gravels and extended maturing in top-quality French oak barriques, has resulted in a surprisingly integrated and harmonious wine with concentrated brambly, berryish, spicy flavours, ideal for something gamey like venison, or exotic like ostrich.

Also hand-harvested and crafted, the Elspeth Syrah comes from Paddy and Tim's original plantings. Dark and fragrant with distinctively deep aromas of plum and pepper seasoned with toasty oak, it bursts with intense blackcurrant, plum and pepper flavours, making a complex, concentrated wine with supple tannins and a spicy, sustained finish which is made for pepper steak or something similarly spicy!

The Prestons don't just use wine from their own vineyard in their search for the perfect wine to bear the Elspeth label. Two boutique vineyards boasting differing soils, microclimates and low vine yields were specially selected to produce the stunning Elspeth Chardonnay, a refined and exceptionally complex wine with ripe, mouth-filling peach, pear and citrus flavours resulting in a rich, long, crisp finish. Already delicious, it's great with seafood or creamy chicken and will flourish with a little cellaring.

vineyard

Moffat Road, Mills Reef's stunning Art Deco inspired HQ in the Bay of Plenty, was completed in 1995. Hawke's Bay, where the vineyards are, was once considered the Art Deco capital of the world, as much of Napier was rebuilt in the style after much of the city was levelled by an earthquake in 1931.

Frequently acclaimed as one of the most beautiful and stylish buildings - let alone wineries! - in New Zealand, the complex boasts winemaking and bottling facilities, an enormous 500 barrel cellar, and spacious and gracious wine tasting areas where you can also make cellar door purchases from the inimitable "maestro" Oliver Pasquale, whose encyclopaedic knowledge of Mills Reef's extensive wine list is unmatched. Whether you have a lot of knowledge or a little, you'll always walk out of the cellar door with a smile on your face - and feeling you've learnt a little bit more.

There's also an award-winning restaurant which caters for all tastes from its Pacific-style A La Carte menu - all ideal matches for Mills Reef's prize-winning wines.

Mills Reef Winery and Restaurant
143 Moffat Road, Bethlehem, Tauranga
ph: [64 7] 576 8800   NZ Freephone: 0800 64 55 77
info@millsreef.co.nz   www.millsreef.co.nz
Cellar Door: Open 10am - 5pm Daily

3 brothers winery

3 brothers winery

kristian, adam and jacob nooyen - chef, winemaker, marketing, whiz-kid… and party animals!

They come from adventurous stock, these boys: half Croatian, half Dutch. Over a hundred years ago, their illustrious forebear, Ivan Milicich Senior, jumped in the deep end and left his homeland in faraway Croatia, bringing with him Waikato's first vines and founding one of New Zealand's oldest and most renowned wineries. On the Dutch side of the family, their paternal grandfather, Martinus Nooyen, took a bet with one of his nine brothers that he would never leave the Netherlands for New Zealand, but he did over 60 years ago. His son Pieter Nooyen, a musician of some note, met the beautiful Nelda Milicich on a blind date, before helping her and her family build their little vineyard into the wine, food and entertainment destination it has become… and in the midst of all this, they produced three sons. Jacob's the winemaker, energetic Kristian's the chef, and irrepressible Adam's in charge of marketing, they're all in the same boat, often doing each other's jobs, helping each other to make the best wines and having the most fun they can.

In terms of decision making do you get more say because you're the oldest, Jacob?
Jacob: You'd think 'cos I'm the oldest I'd be the boss, but it hasn't worked out that way! The decision-making for each department falls on the person responsible. Of course, I get the biggest say in the winery, Kristian in the kitchen and Adam for the marketing -
Kristian: But we all help each other…
Adam: When Kristian's busy in the kitchen, I'll help out, and Jacob'll help me with marketing ideas: it's good to experience all aspects of the business - it helps you keep on track with how everything's going.

Is there much competitiveness between you boys?
Jacob: Only when it comes to wakeboarding -
Kristian: Or tennis…
Adam: Or shooting, golf, playing music! Because I'm six years younger, I try to beat them at everything.
Kristian: "Try's" the operative word!
Jacob: Or is that just "trying" (laughs)

Is there a particular vintage experience you remember?
Jacob: I was stuck in the back of a very large van full of grapes with two amorous old ladies who tried to take advantage of me - (laughter around the table). We'd done a promotional stomping and I'd collapsed in the back of the van half-asleep when I woke up to find them at it! I yelled to my mate driving the van to pull over before I ran for my life down the street covered in grapes… it was quite traumatic - they were really old!
Kristian: We used to have a 300 kilo press and it took forever, so we bought a three tonne press off friends and the others filled it up and turned it on and then everyone left. Except the machine stopped at 2am and I was stuck inside it, trying to clean it after catering for 200 people! I'll never forget it - and hope I don't have to do it again…
Adam: He's miffed because we weren't there.

Where were you?
Jacob: Um, I had something on…
Kristian: They were partying in Auckland, the bastards!

Do you all have the same taste in music?
Jacob: Yes, we all have similar tastes in music - we also play old school rock in a band together.
Kristian: It's called the 3 Brothers' Band, of course (laughs)!
Adam: I sing and play guitar; Kristian plays the drums; and Jacob plays everything else - keyboards, harmonica and sax.

Where can people see you play?
Adam: Every Sunday lunch at the Vilagrad winery! Or else hotels and venues in Waiheke Island, Taupo, Rotorua, Hamilton and Auckland. We'll play anywhere we're

booked, whatever party we're invited to. We always have our instruments out at family gatherings and parties.
Kristian: Actually, weddings and conferences, mainly…

Best wine tosser story?
Adam: We once held a wedding here at the winery and this guy came in and he refused to drink our wine, so he brought his own. So we opened it up at the bar and tipped it out and poured our own wine in the bottle and he loved it!

Do you have any other interests apart from winemaking?
Kristian: I enjoy scuba diving, fishing, motorbike riding, music, barbecues, wake boarding, skiing and snowboarding… one time I went diving for scallops and when I got back to the surface, I was in the middle of a pod of orcas - it was amazing!
Jacob: I'm exactly the same as Kristian - and I like having sex.
Adam: When you can get it (laughs)! I go fly fishing with my girlfriend's dad and we have to throw them all back because they're only doing it for sport. If I want to take one home, I have to kill it when they're not watching…

wine

Despite their fun-loving, hard-partying attitude to life, these are busy boys! In addition to making the wine for 3 Brothers, Jacob is also winemaker for the family winery, Vilagrad Wines, one of New Zealand's oldest, with vines originally planted 100 years ago by his great-grandfather, Ivan Milicich Senior. It's a family affair, presided over by their wonderful mum, Ivan's grand-daughter Nelda, and their indefatigable dad Pieter.

"It's pretty rare to find such a close, cohesive relationship in a winery: we've always helped each other out, striving together to make not just the best wine from its optimal region, but matching it perfectly to food. Jacob and I will brainstorm the best dishes for the wine together," says Kristian, who's influenced by his mum and grandmother, with all their wonderful Croatian and Mediterranean food. That extends to the wine, making only five wines from the regions best suited to them: Chardonnay from Gisborne, Merlot from Hawke's Bay, and Waikato from their own small vineyard.

"Malbec has such a mouth-gripping, pizza-eating taste," says Jacob. "I love it!" Hand-harvested by the boys from their own vineyard, 3 Brothers Malbec is redolent of grandma's homemade jam, the nose displaying cinnamon and liquorice aromas, with distinctively robust tannins and intense, rustically earthy flavours. "This wine deserves food," says Kristian. "Especially Mediterranean cuisine like marinated fetta and olives, calzone and mozzarella."

Grown and hand harvested by the Kingsbeer family in Gisborne, 3 Brothers Chardonnay has been hand-crafted by Jacob to create a well-balanced and elegant wine with concentrated flavours, with aromas of hazelnut, almond and rockmelon, and layered with mandarin and hints of ripe grapefruit, finished by notes of light French oak. Kristian reckons it's "Beautiful with crisp garden salads, rich, creamy pasta, char-grilled prawns or smoked chicken."

Grown and hand harvested by the Bunny family in Masterton, Wairarapa, 3 Brothers Pinot Noir is "sexy and seductive, just like me!" according to Adam. With redolent aromas of cherry liqueur chocolate, ripe raspberries and notes of spicy red peppercorn, it's layered with seasoned oak and finely structured tannins, making it perfect for rich, gamey dishes such as sage-stuffed duck, braised quail, emu steaks or tuna tartare. Mmmmmm….

vineyard

Set on a beautiful estate surrounded by vines, Vilagrad Winery is home to 3 brothers - the siblings and the wine label - adding a dash of funky, youthful energy to one of New Zealand's oldest family-run wineries, with the contributions of each generation built on by the next.

Enjoy Kristian's delicious Mediterranean-style cuisine, perfectly matched to Jacob's award-winning wines for Sunday lunch, while the boys entertain you on stage! Call ahead to reserve tastings and winery tours - and one of Kristian's famous platters, groaning with delicacies like home smoked salmon and chicken, marinated feta, and selection of home baked breads, pesto, hummus, marinated kebabs and much more…

3 Brothers Winery
702 Rukuhia Road, RD2 Ohaupo, Hamilton
ph: [64 7] 825 2893
wines@3brothers.co.nz   www.3brothers.co.nz
Cellar Door : Open Daily 9am - 5pm; Sunday Lunch 12pm - 4pm   Tours, tasting and platters by appointment.

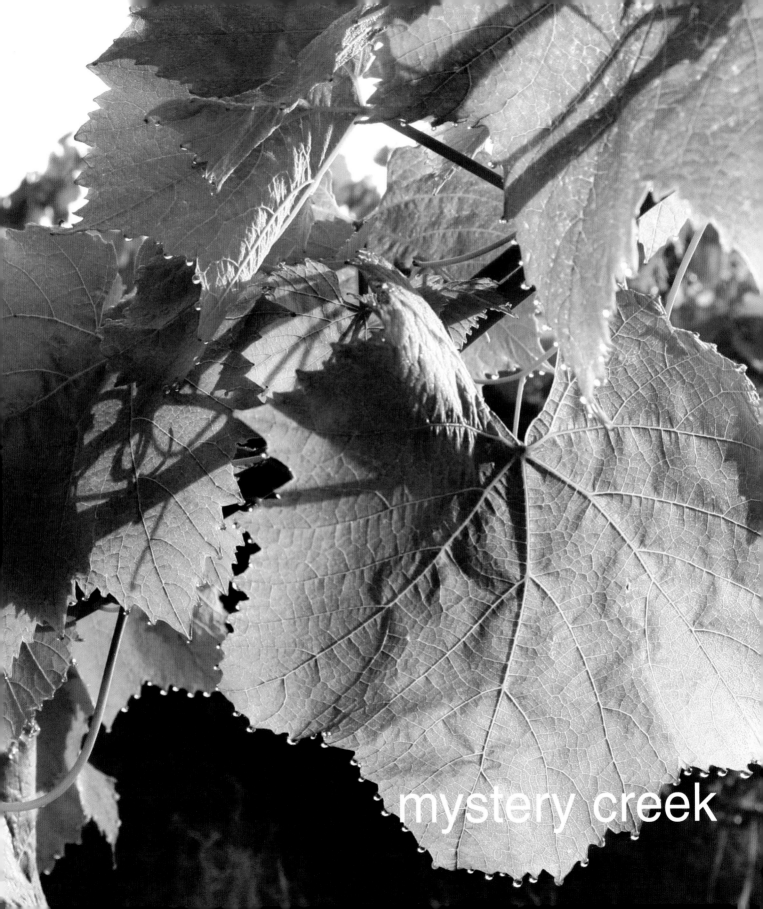

mystery creek

mystery creek

garry major and neil redgrave - winemakers

They're the Odd Couple, Garry and Neil: one thoughtful and laconic, with a dry sense of humour (that's Garry); the other an ebullient bundle of energy full of enthusiasm and funny stories (that's Neil). And yet, they somehow work together. Neil tells a great story about once accidentally blending two tanks of Riesling: one sweet and one super sweet. A recipe for disaster, but somehow ending up with a swag of Gold Medals. You could say Garry and Neil are the same - though we'll leave it to you to decide who's sweeter!

Despite being such different characters, together they're responsible for some of the best wines in New Zealand. Mystery Creek was founded by Garry in 1993 after he left Villa Maria Wines and realised "it was too expensive to go out and buy a bottle every day. So I thought I'd start my own winery... I mean, you have to drink a lot to be a good winemaker, right?"

Neil joined three years later after becoming a winemaker on "doctor's orders". How so? "Well, I worked on an oil rig for five years and had to get off for health reasons. I got a summer job as a cellar hand, then got my qualifications, then worked for a number of different places in NZ and overseas." As he puts it with a laugh, "I've done the big and the small; the good, the bad and the ugly..."

Speaking of which, Neil once "mooned" curmudgeonly former PM Robert "Piggy" Muldoon. "He was driving past and it just seemed the right thing to do. Hey, I was young!"

Still, he and Garry seem to be doing something right: starting with their renowned Barrel Ferment Chardonnay winning the prestigious and very competitive Liquorland Top 100, they and their wines have gone on to win even more acclaim, regularly collecting prizes for their power and grace. You could say as a result, the Mystery Creek teams are, well, over the moon...

What do you like least about your job?
Garry: Paperwork - and the computer!
Neil: Fixing other people's cock-ups!

Is there a major goal you'd like to achieve before you stop stomping grapes?
Garry: I'd like to win a gold medal for our Pinot.
Neil: I'd like to retire on my own vineyard.

Art vs science in winemaking - your thoughts?
Garry: When things go wrong it's down to science and when they go right, it's art.
Neil: It's not art for art's sake anymore: you do have to have the qualifications too. The trick's getting the blend between the two right. For example, we don't have a pH metre here (which measures wines' acidity). Most of our assessments are done on taste and other parameters. And we usually get it right!

How many bottles in your cellar?
Garry: About 250 - mostly Kiwi whites and Aussie reds.
Neil: Mate, I'm always broke! It depends on how many of 'em are mine, but generally I'm pretty hopeless at saving wine - or money!

Have you ever drunk cask wine?
Garry: Yes, and it was bloody horrible, but it was all I could afford at the time.
Neil: Sure! It was crap, but it was cheap and cheerful at the time. Any Kiwi who tells you they didn't drink out of a cask in the 70s is lying!

What music do you listen to at work?
Garry: I try to enjoy the silence, but Neil listens to heavy rock which drives me up the wall -
Neil: It's classic rock, mate! You know, Gary Moore, Pink Floyd, that sort of stuff...

Best wine tosser story?

Garry: I've been lucky not to come across that many, and to be honest, I wouldn't drink with them anyway.

Neil: I remember when Penfolds amalgamated with Montana and made their champagne here, they had a big press shindig in a posh Auckland hotel for their first release. They brought in some snooty Frenchman in a dinner jacket and cravat who berated us Kiwis for not opening champagne properly. As he was talking about the right angle to hold it and all that, a girl walked past holding a magnum. He grabbed it off her and kept going on with a story about how the bottle should sigh gently after it's been opened, just like a woman you've made love to. Anyway, he opens it, the cork takes off, hits the light fixture above him, breaks it and shatters it all over him. He's standing there stunned while wine gushes everywhere. And then someone in the crowd puts his hand up and yells "I KNOW that woman!"

Who would you most like to share a glass of wine with?

Garry: Tiger Woods, because I'm keen on golf.

Neil: Elle McPherson - do I need to give a reason?

Do you have kids?

Garry: Two - Ben's 16 and he's in the US at the moment. Sam's 18 and she's a winemaker in Marlborough.

Neil: Two as well - my son's 13 and my daughter's 10.

Would you encourage them into winemaking?

Garry: Sure! Sam's interested because she worked in the vineyard and helped in the winery at vintage, and she completed the same course I did at Gisborne. She seems really keen on it.

Neil: Probably not. My daughter was heading in that direction, but she's very artistic.

What would your last meal be - and what wine would go with it?

Garry: A huge plate of fresh scallops with a bottle of Montrachet.

Neil: A nice, fresh, juicy East Coast crayfish with a nice bottle of Chardonnay - like our Barrel Ferment Chardy, which is a beauty.

What's distinctive about your label?

Neil: Well, it's not a mystery! It's all about the best possible, most distinctive wine for anyone to enjoy.

wine

They love Chardonnay at the Creek, and with good reason. The spectacular Barrel Ferment Chardonnay won the Liquorland Top 100 in 2000. "It really put us on the map," Garry says proudly. And deservedly so: this is a voluptuous and powerful wine with soft tropical flavours and elegantly subtle oak overtones, it was cold-fermented in both French and American oak barrels, resulting in a refined and balance wine for Chardonnay lovers. With a slightly mealy backbone and hints of caramel, it'll develop beautifully over the next couple of years. But you can enjoy it now with almost anything, from ripe, soft cheeses to fruity or creamy puds!

Grown on the Home Block, right next to the winery, the Waikato Sauvignon Blanc is the result of a "perfect vintage", and it's no mystery why! With an abundance of ripe passionfruit and gooseberry aromas, this rich and opulent wine is layered with ripe tropical fruit and an underlying minerality that Neil hopes is typical of the Home Block, with its gentle sun and sandy soil. Garry reckons it's ideal with scallops in a rich Mornay sauce.

"When we eventually hit the jackpot with Pinot, I'll really be chuffed," says Garry, and, given his laconic nature, that's saying something. And the Waikato Block 3 Pinot Noir shows how serious he is about getting it right. Harvested from three local vineyards, and helped along by a low-yielding, higher quality vintage, this exuberant wine exhibits a strong, savoury and spicy nose, and bursts with ripe cherry and berry flavours balanced by silky, well-integrated tannins and a subtle underlying savoury smokiness. A wonderful food wine, especially with game, tomato-based dishes or a nice, thick, beef fillet.

cellar door

Set on 22 acres of olde English gardens and native groves by the river, Mystery Creek is a must-see destination, especially with the locals, who all flock to The Woodbox, run by former Regional Café Owner of the Year, Matt Cooper. "The motto's 'You All Fit In", says Matt with a laugh. "Whether it's the couple enjoying a romantic candle-lit dinner, high-powered business meetings, Nana's 70th, or Mum, Dad and 2.4 kids - arriving on tractors for a beer or glass of wine, on horseback for a coffee or by boat for a winery tour - everybody's welcome!"

Featuring a Manuka Wood-fired Oven, you can enjoy everything from a casual café lunch and wood-fired pizzas through to a six-course Degustation Winemakers' Dinner, featuring dishes perfectly matched to Mystery Creek's portfolio of exceptional wines.

Mystery Creek Wines
Mystery Creek Road, RD1 Ohaupo
ph: [64 7] 823 6464
sales@mysterycreekwines.co.nz   www.mysterycreekwines.co.nz
Cellar Door: Open 10am - 5pm Wednesday - Sunday
The Woodbox Restaurant: Open 11am - 11.30pm Wednesday - Sunday. Closed Monday and Tuesday, except Public Holidays.

judge valley

judge valley

kevin geraghty - proprietor and winegrower

"Dad was God, and Dad was a farmer," says Kevin Geraghty of his passion for farming. "I always wanted to follow in his footsteps." A knockabout bloke with a wicked sense of humour, he was a dairy farmer for years before planting Judge Valley's first vines in 1997. "Dairy farming was a bit 'been there, done that'" he reckons. But how did he make the swap to winegrowing? A pie and beer man from way back, he suspects it might have had something to do with serving sacramental wine as a good little altar boy. And learning French, which resulted in a lifelong love of French village life and the joy of vintage there.

"But my knowledge (when I started planting) was so minimal you wouldn't believe it! I didn't know that Merlot wine came from a Merlot vine - I thought "Merlot" was a brand name just like "XXXX" or something!" Luckily, he knew enough to plant on north-facing slope, leading up to his homestead, where from about six in the evening, you'll find him out in the Jacuzzi with a glass of good wine, enjoying the view. He hasn't looked back since. And luckily, he knows a lot more about winegrowing now, producing some of New Zealand's best Bordeaux in a small wine region which isn't that well-known, but on the strength of Judge Valley's award-winning Bordeaux, is bound to get better known!

What are the differences between dairy farming and winegrowing?
In a social sense, winegrowing's a lot less restrictive - you don't have to be home to milk the vines at 4 o'clock every day, so you can go out and have a life. Thank God the vines can look after 'emselves!

Do you still run dairy cattle on your property?
No, thank God! Although I planted my first vines in 1997, I kept the herd for four years, working both jobs - tending the vines and milking the cows. But then the vines kinda took over my imagination and my enthusiasm, and when I get interested, I can get a bit obsessed… so I sold the cows in 2001, and since then, the only animals here now are the dog… and me!

What's one of the hardest things about being a winemaker?
The waiting's the hardest, but I guess that's just a mind thing. My wine's not commercial: it's made to improve in the bottle and shouldn't be opened for at least a year or two after bottling. Bottling's a year after harvest, which means, if you started pruning in 2005, you're not even tasting the finished product for at least four years after you started growing it! Four years from vine to glass! That's hard, mate! I'm just a greedy bugger and I generally slug a bottle coming home from the bottling. To hell with this waiting business!

What made you choose Bordeaux-style wines as opposed to Merlot?
Being a country boy, I tended to eat more country-style meals like steak and eggs and Bordeaux style wines went well with that. So I decided that if I was going to be a winegrower, I'd plant vines that made wines I wanted to drink.

How many bottles in your cellar?
Seven - can you believe it? And my cellar - if you could call it that - only consists of my wine. I've been so dedicated and devoted to getting my vineyard and label up and running, I haven't had any time to go out sampling or buying other great wines. Basically I've got six or seven special bottles which I've actually managed to save - usually I just drink it when I get it. But one day, I'm going to build myself a cellar and go collect some wine and actually store it for a while before I drink it. One day…

What do you do to relax?
Well, I've got a spa parked out on my front lawn, and at about six or seven every evening, I go out and get in there with the radio on and a bottle of my wine and bliss out under the stars. Beautiful! I used to read in there, but books and spas don't go so well together!

What's your party trick?

My party trick's causing me serious pain at the moment! No matter where I go, I end up dancing on the table. I've been kicked out of pubs, bars and clubs all over the world for dancing on tables! Last week, I was dancing on the bar in our new function centre and lost my balance and fell onto the concrete floor - nearly broke my ankle, and I was on crutches for five days!

What's the strangest job you've ever had apart from winemaking?

I once worked at a sock factory when I worked at a bank (before I started farming). Being young blokes, we basically spent all our pay on grog, so I had to get another job to keep my car going! I worked part-time from six to ten at night in the factory. There was a conveyor belt with fabricated steel legs with a foot at the top. As the conveyor came past, you put a sock on a foot as it went through a steam press, and a guy on the other side of the conveyor'd take the sock off the foot, fold it into a pair and put it away. That's all we did all night. Totally and utterly mind-numbing. But I didn't need to buy a pair of socks for years!

Who's your winemaker?

The amazing Shayne Cox of Corazon Winery in West Auckland. He's had years and years of experience with Bordeaux-style wines, and as a result, that's exclusively my wine too. Plus, of course, it goes great with steak and eggs, eh? Anyway, I grow everything here and send all the fruit to Shane and he works his magic with it, and then I get it back when it's all nicely packaged with my label on it. I just have to remember to stop drinking it straight away!

wine

Given Kevin's love of Malbec and Bordeaux-style wines, it's no surprise that his wines are all blends of Cabernet Franc, Merlot and Malbec. "What's so distinctive about my label is that I'm growing some of New Zealand's best red wines in a totally unfashionable area," says Kevin, but his wines are hardly unfashionable, being enjoyed in some of New Zealand's best restaurants, and enjoying wide acclaim.

Judge Valley's award-winning Cottage Block Cabernet Franc/Merlot/Malbec, recipient of four stars in Cuisine Magazine and a Silver Medal in the Liquorland Top 100, is a promisingly rich, purple-flushed wine with a fragrant, spicy bouquet and loads of ripe, brambly, slightly chocolate notes, with the Malbec adding a touch of gaminess, and enjoyable right now, especially with Italian food, red meat - "or a lovely red-head," says Kevin.

The Limited Edition Cabernet Franc/Merlot/Malbec is a deeply coloured, fragrant and vibrantly fruity red, full of Cab Franc's typically brambly, spicy flavour. With supple tannins and oaky complexity, it will develop more complexity and finish with age, and is great

with rich meaty dishes like osso bucco "and a blonde companion," adds Kevin.

The Summer Rain Cabernet Franc/Merlot/Malbec is so-called because "it's got the same sense of pleasure and relief you get when it rains at the end of a hot summer's day," says Kevin. Fruity and supple, with a sweet oak influence, it has warm plum and spice flavours, exhibiting very good depth. It's enjoyable now, but if you can be more patient than its maker, with careful cellaring, it'll reward you with even more depth and complexity. It's made for spicy foods or Brazilian churrasco barbecue. "And Annie Lennox, please!" says Kevin.

vineyard

"Wine's for fun - you're not meant to get all heavy and scientific about it," says Kevin, and that party-loving spirit's embodied in Judge Valley's regular events, especially Vino @ the Valley, an afternoon of music in the vineyard, held every Sunday. As well as enjoying music from local bands, you can also enjoy a selection of gourmet platters with your wine.

And as well as the (in)famous spa, Judge Valley now boasts a brand new function centre crafted from cedar and local river stone and finished in black, copper and natural tones, it's designed to complement the spectacular Waikato landscape. Kevin's especially proud of it: "People come and look at it for their wedding and straight away sign on the dotted line because it's so distinctive."

And if you've had a bit too much of a good time, why not spend the night - or weekend! - at the Cabernet Chalet, Judge Valley's own exclusive getaway, with uninterrupted views of the hills and vines. And your own private spa, just like Kevin's, and a complimentary bottle of bubbly to enjoy when you're in!

Judge Valley Vineyard
178 Judge Road, Puahue RD1, Te Awamutu
ph: [64 7] 872 1821   Freephone: 0800 2 JUDGE VALLEY
info@judgevalley.co.nz   www.judgevalley.co.nz

mission estate

mission estate

paul mooney - winemaker

Founded in 1851 by Marist Fathers from an earlier missionary outpost, Mission Estate's had a long and eventful history, including flood, fire and earthquake. Talk about acts of God! In 1909, the magnificent Grande Maison - or Big House - where the Fathers had made their home since 1880 (and which is now Mission Estate's Tourism and Hospitality Centre), was cut into twelve pieces and moved on rollers to the higher ground where it now rests after disastrous floods. The journey took two days.

In 1931, disaster struck. A massive earthquake, measuring a phenomenal 7.9 on the Richter scale struck Napier and Hawke's Bay, levelling much of the area, including the Mission. Two priests and seven seminary students meditating in the chapel were killed when it was reduced to rubble in the quake.

"But there aren't any ghosts," Paul Mooney, Mission Estate's unflappable winemaker says. "Though sometimes late at night, it can be a bit spooky down in the cellar." And Mission Estate's wine, harvested from some of New Zealand's oldest vines, are so good it's almost scary. Right, Paul? "Well, I wouldn't say that - it's a bit corny, isn't it?" Um, okay. What would you say, then? "They'll make the earth move for you! Ha ha ha!"

How did you get into winemaking?
I met John Cuttance, the previous winemaker, way back in the 70s, and at the time he was looking for a new assistant winemaker. I'd been to uni and done a Physics degree, and was thinking about whether or not to go back and do a Masters. I had to decide whether to do the Degree or take the winemaking job, and luckily for me, I got the job. I didn't have any vintage or winemaking experience at the time but the whole prospect of making wine seemed really interesting.

Tell us about sustainable winemaking.
Well, we've always tried to do things here in a sustainable way - partly because back in the 80s we had to treat our own winery waste, so I always knew how to do it. I've always tended to look at ways to do things cost effectively, and that usually means doing it in an environmentally sustainable way. For example, our refrigeration system's designed with the environment in mind, with very strict controls and tight management.

Now, we've got the ISO 1401 system, which although it means a bit more day-to-day management paperwork, and can sometimes pull you away from the winemaking, it's a necessary evil.

Is there much camaraderie between winemakers in your region?
Yes - there are a few of us who've been around since the "early days" in the 80s and we get together from time to time.

Is there much competitiveness?
Although there's some natural competitiveness, we Hawke's Bay wineries like to market our wine as a region. So in that way, there's probably more cooperation than competition - in fact, our main competitors are probably Aussies!

What's the worst disaster at vintage?
Last vintage we got a new conveyor system for the grape waste which removes grape stalks. It tied itself into a big knot, knocking us out of production for three nerve-racking days!

Do you have any nicknames in the vineyard?
I've got the sort of personality that if I'm really busy with our winemaking I get really focused. The winemaking problems tend to take over and everyone can't get answers out of me. The guys in the cellar call me Moons 'cos they think I'm moonstruck. It's affectionate… I hope!

paul mooney

Corks vs screw tops?
Well, I think corks have a lot to offer and a good bottle with a good cork makes for great wine. We've done heaps of trials and found that after two or three years, a wine under cork is often more interesting. Under screw caps wines sometimes don't develop the same interesting secondary characters.

What's your favourite hangover cure?
Beer. I make my own home brew: a nice, dry, low-alcohol lager, which is very refreshing. And great for a hangover!

Who's the most interesting person you've shared a glass of wine with?
Francois de Ligneris, who I worked with during vintage in '85 at Chateaux Soutard, in St. Emillon. His family had been there for two centuries, and although most people in the area were deeply conservative, he and his family were fiercely liberal. He'd studied architecture and had an amazing sense of style.

The Ligerises were way ahead of their time, developing sustainable methods in their vineyards even then. You could see the difference: while everyone else's vines looked tired by harvest time, theirs looked green and lush. That's been an inspiration for me to see our Gimblett Gravels vineyards farmed in a similarly sustainable way.

What's the strangest job you've ever had apart from winemaking?
I worked for a year in a scientific base station in Antarctica as a geophysics technician, with ten other guys. It was amazing - obviously very isolated, and the way we lived our lives was very simple. It was like being dumped back in time into the Nineteenth Century.

If you could be anyone else, who would you be?
I guess I'd be something completely different, like a missionary (!). Or maybe a doctor who worked in Africa and did something that improved other peoples' lives. Or else a great cricketer like Glen McGrath, though I'd have to bowl like him, wouldn't I?

wine
Producing ten grape varieties at different vineyards around Hawke's Bay, as well as sourcing from specially selected premium vineyards, Mission Estate produces a winning wine for every occasion, from the superb value Estate range through to the flagship Jewelstone collection.

Mission Estate's Estate range offers affordable premium reds and whites, which though perfect for everyday drinking, enjoy all the complexity and refinement of more expensive wines. With typically Pinot Gris pear and apple fruit characters, the soft and approachable Estate Pinot Gris is nonetheless rich and intense with a full round mouth feel. Although eminently quaffable now, it'll gain even further intensity and complexity in a year or two. A trendy summer wine to enjoy with an alfresco lunch of light chicken salad.

Mission Reserve wines are produced from the finest quality grapes, and hand-crafted as the perfect accompaniment to fine food. Mission Estate built its reputation on fine wine, and the Mission Reserve Syrah represents its long heritage beautifully. Deep and vibrant, it's got peppery aromatic notes, showing luscious dark berry flavours with spicy undertones. Made for drinking now and to enjoy with a peppered steak or venison, it'll develop over the next two years.

The renowned Jewelstone selection is noted for its intensity and finesse. A refined aroma of discreet oak - a result of its brand new, fine-grained barrels - imbues this full-bodied wine with a silky mouthfeel and a long, elegant finish. It's the perfect match for poultry or fish mornay and with careful cellaring over the next three to five years, will become even creamier and complex.

vineyard

New Zealand's oldest vineyard, dating back to 1851, when it was founded by Marist Fathers who established the Mission from which it gets its name, Mission Estate's colonial-style St Mary's Mission building has recently been extensively restored. Don't miss visiting the cellar in the original homestead, the glorious Le Grand Maison, where you can make exclusive cellar door purchases and enjoy them with the exquisite, award-winning cuisine of the award-winning Mission Restaurant - along with sweeping views of Napier and the coast beyond.

After enjoying lunch or dinner on the sun-drenched terrace, take a stroll through the beautifully manicured gardens, or take a tour of the winery, which showcase the Mission's long and eventful history: earthquakes, fires, floods... and maybe even a ghost or two?

Mission Estate Winery
198 Church Road, Greenmeadows, Napier, Hawke's Bay
ph: [64 6] 845 9350
missionwinery@clear.net.nz   www.missionestate.co.nz
Cellar Door: Open 9am to 5pm Monday to Saturday and 10am to 4pm Sunday
Extended hours from Labour Weekend until Easter
Winery Tours from 10.30am to 2pm

sacred hill

sacred hill

tony bish - winemaker and david mason - managing director

After more than a century of successful farming, the Mason family started planting grapes on their magnificent estate Dartmoor in 1982. David, Sacred Hill's energetic managing director, laughs about those early roots:

"Being virtually unpaid slave labour for my parents, when I was a student and we planted our first vineyard, we could drink two or three good bottles of wine a night, but we were only paid five bucks an hour - a very dangerous predicament for a wine drinker! So Tony Bish, the winemaker, my brother Mark and I decided to make more great wine than we could drink. And that's how Sacred Hill was born, with 350 cases of barrel-fermented Sauvignon Blanc, the fantastic '86 vintage…"

Despite its phenomenal growth, David and Tony have not compromised their own impeccable standards - nor changed much since Sacred Hill's inception all those years ago: most of the original team are still on board, and still committed to hand-crafting the best wines they can. Named after the nearby hamlet of Puketapu - which means "sacred hill" in Maori - David and Tony have scaled lofty heights of excellence without losing that youthful enthusiasm and fun, resulting in a label renowned not only for its great wines but its vibrant personality and culture - and its great parties over the years!

Both Tony and David love the Hawke's Bay lifestyle, whether at the beach or on horseback. In addition to being a talented winemaker, Tony and associates also manufactures their own cheeses (including Te Mata Cape Kidnappers Brie, Te Mata Pacifica Sheep's Milk Blue and Te Mata Pania Vine Ashe Brie among them) with the help of talented French fromagier Jean-Luc Danquigny - the ideal accompaniment to Sacred Hill's award-winning wines.

It might sound cheesy, but though you might lead a horse to the Sacred Hill winery but you won't need to make it drink!

How did you get into winemaking?
Tony: I fell into it, really. I was at Auckland University doing Law and after two years of hating it, I decided to bail out. I went and lived on a Gisborne beach with my girlfriend at the time and had a fabulous summer being a beach bum - until we ran out of money! I had the option of working in the local freezing works (abattoir) or a winery. And the winery sounded much nicer!

What do you love best about what you do?
Tony: We bottle fun! We take a lot of pride in what we do, but in the end, it's just a beverage to enjoy with family and friends. It's a great opportunity to pack something that'll blow people away into a bottle. That's at the heart of it really, I love that.

What makes a good winemaker?
David: The tenacity of a farmer to take the whims of the weather in your stride, and the passion of an artist to never be satisfied with the wines you've made to date.
Tony: That elusive combination of experience, knowledge and passion…

Tell us about the cheese-making…
Tony: After travelling through Europe and seeing all the wonderful cheeses in those amazing wine regions, my wife Karryn and I thought we had to have a good cheese to really make Hawke's Bay "proper" wine country. We'd talked a lot about it, and after we got the youngest of our four kids off to school, we thought it was now or never…

Do you get much conversation out of cheese-making?
Tony: Yeah, more and more. People are fascinated by the obvious combination of wine and cheese, and we love the dictum of having cholesterol in your cheese, and red wine to clear your arteries out again!

tony bish and david mason

What's your favourite cheese?
Tony: I love Rocquefort. But although we aren't allowed to make un-pasteurised cheese in New Zealand, we do make one in that style.

What did you want to be as a kid?
Tony: A pilot… but I found another way of getting high!

What do you do to relax?
Tony: I love going down the beach, surfing and boogie boarding with the kids - or else, skiing.
David: Riding and heli-skiing, which has to be the greatest indulgence a man can have!

What pets do you have?
Tony: We've got a Fox Terrier-Jack Russell cross called Dolly.
David: Eight horses, two dogs, a revolving number of cats… and a mother-in-law!

Who's the most interesting person you've shared a glass of wine with?
David: It'd have to be Denis Dubourdieau, the wizard of Bordeaux white wine, and long-time head of Bordeaux University's Wine Department. I did a vintage with him back in 1987 at his home, Chateau Reynon. The dinner table was always thronged with some of the best winemakers in France, from some of its greatest chateaux. And for a struggling, non-smoking novice starting to develop his palate, it was fascinating to do comparative tastings with a crowd of Gauloise puffing chain-smokers!

wine

"I love Syrah," says Tony. "It just reminds me of sinking into a big deep leather chair in front of a bearskin rug, toasted by a roaring winter's fire." What a wonderful way to describe Sacred Hill's Deerstalkers Syrah, a stunning hand-picked, small-batch wine with intensely complex aromas of ripe plum, overlaid with classically spicy nuances. A very silky, lusciously indulgent palate of ripe berries and lingering spicy complexity makes this stunning wine perfect for any game or wild meat such as duck, pheasant or venison ("I love venison!" exclaims Tony), accompanied by roasted vegetables and a rich sauce. Or try it with fragrantly spicy Moroccan dishes for an exotic change!

When asked what the worst bit of advice he'd ever received, Tony replies "Someone once told me not to make Sauvignon Blanc, because nobody likes it." Huh? Luckily for us, he didn't follow such spurious advice! Sacred Hill's Marlborough Vineyards Sauvignon Blanc

is a beautifully balanced aromatic wine bursting with a lively medley of lifted passionfruit, lychee and gooseberry characters. Its rich and mouth-filling palate of abundant tropical fruit flavours of passionfruit, lychee and gooseberry give it a richly textured mid-palate and a lingering, tropical finish.

"Chardonnay's so rich, layered, complex - it just packs so much into the glass!" And the Rifleman's Chardonnay certainly goes off with a bang. Hand-picked from old-vine own-rooted Mendoza Chardonnay vines with naturally low yields and exceptionally intense fruit, this rich and creamy wine has lifted, elegantly sweet citrus and peach aromas with nutty and mealy characters. It explodes in the mouth with ripe peach, roasted almond and sweet citrus flavours which extend into a long, lingering finish with a citrus lift.

vineyard

Quality's never been sacrificed for quantity at Sacred Hill, which stays true to David and Tony's original vision of hand-crafting the most exceptional wines, no matter what. Growing only the best grapes in the regions best suited to them on their small array of boutique vineyards in Hawke's Bay and Marlborough, the many awards, accolades and medals Sacred Hill's range of extraordinary wines reflect those high standards, especially in the state-of-the-art winery, built in 1995 and renowned as one of Hawke's Bay's most advanced and efficient.

Set on the idyllic landscape of Dartmoor Estate, amidst groves of native and exotic trees, with breathtaking views of the spectacular Dartmoor Valley, Sacred Hill's picturesque cellar door is one of Hawke's Bay's most popular wine experiences during summer, offering the opportunity to taste and purchase Sacred Hill's unique wines in a relaxed yet sophisticated ambience.

Sacred Hill Wines
1033 Dartmoor Road, Puketapu, Napier
ph: [64 6] 879 8760   Cellar Door: [64 6] 844 0138
enquiries@sacredhill.com   www.sacredhill.com
Cellar Door: Open Daily 11am - 5pm December - February
Closed Christmas Day and Boxing Day (25 and 26 December); and New Year's Day

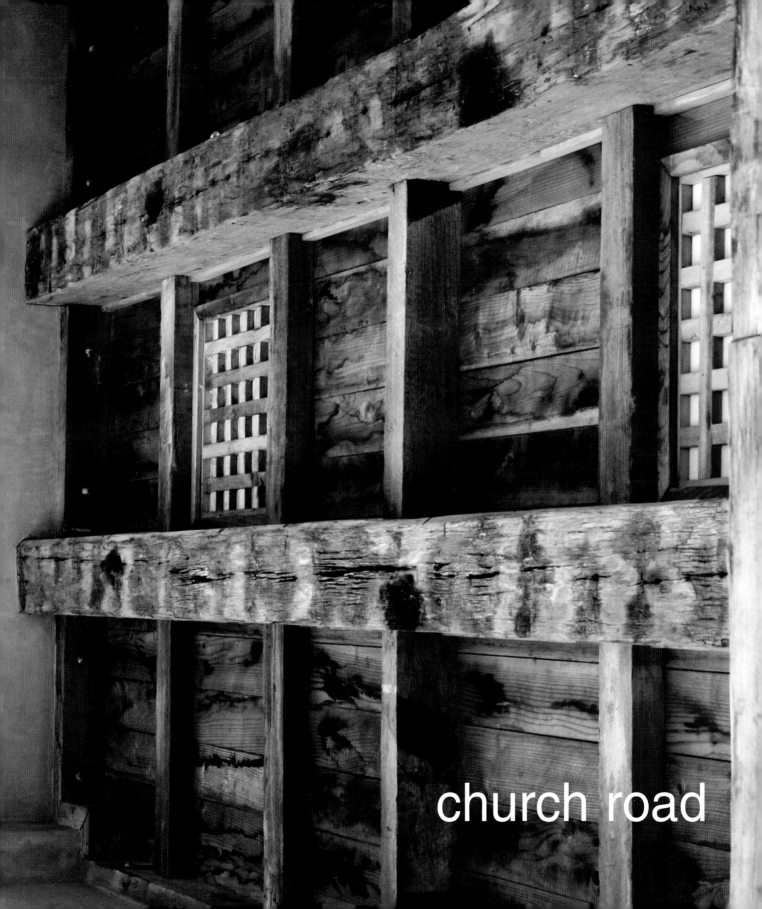

church road

church road

chris scott - winemaker

With a passion for food, wine and the Hawke's Bay lifestyle, Chris found it easy to move from a Business degree into the wine industry. What he didn't find so easy was giving up his love for bogan rock, having once been the lead singer in a rock band called Dazed and Confused, when he didn't just have longer hair, but hair. Music's loss being wine's gain? "Well, not exactly," he says with a laugh. "I don't know how much music lost!"

Chris actually did his first ever vintage at Church Road, before moving to Gisborne to work for Montana Wines. He rejoined Church Road as assistant winemaker in 2002. Now Senior Winemaker responsible for overseeing Church Road's entire wine portfolio, he's constantly striving for "that classic balance between power and elegance", something he achieves in his winemaking, if not necessarily his music-making!

What do you love best about what you do?
Apart from the people in the industry and the team of guys who work here in the winery, the thing that spins my wheels the most is basically anything to do with innovation, new ways of doing things, new grape varieties, new ideas, that sort of thing. We tend to experiment an awful lot, and the successes from those sorts of projects are really rewarding.

What's one of the hardest things about being a winemaker?
The time away from family, particularly during vintage, and then outside vintage, the marketing work you're required to travel a reasonable amount, and with a young family at home it takes a fair bit of time out of your year.

Is your partner involved in the wine industry?
She's probably one of our biggest consumers! (laughs)

Is there a particular vintage experience you remember?
Probably my favourite vintage story from the last few years would be when we went out to the vineyard and I asked the vineyard manager how things were and he said "I've had a shitter of a day!" Basically, he lived ages away from the vineyard, and his wife had gotten a flat tyre, so he'd had to drive home to change it for her. While he was there, our neighbour rang to tell him his travelling irrigator had just gone out of control and wrapped itself around something. So he rushed back out to work, and when he got there, discovered one of the pickers had gotten caught short and relieved themselves in the pumphouse. Enraged, he'd grabbed the Portaloo and drove it into the middle of the driveway so nobody could possibly miss it... It was at this point I asked him how his day was. And as he was telling me just how shit it'd been, his assistant drove up in the tractor with four picking bins on the front so she couldn't really see where she was going and drove straight into the Portaloo at 20 k's an hour! Luckily no-one was in it at the time - they'd just gotten out after "restocking" the loo rolls...

What's your favourite drinking game?
I think being a socially responsible winemaker and promoting responsible drinking, I'm not at liberty to play them - and besides, if I have more than three drinks, I'll fall over anyway, so drinking games aren't really my forte!

How many bottles in your cellar?
Not many - most of the wine I bring home hardly hits the kitchen bench before the top gets ripped off by my wife!

Do you make wine with your wife in mind?
I'm probably a bit selfish, actually! (laughs) - I tend to steer wines towards the styles I like drinking.

chris scott

What music do you listen to during vintage?
Well, I'm a bit of a bogan at heart and I still listen to rock music, which is my staple diet.

Though I tend not to listen to too much music while I'm working because I struggle to do more than one thing at a time - and it's a bit of a challenge - my wife tells me it's a man thing!

Is the cellar stereo democratic?
The other guys tend to listen to the local radio station, the Rock, which gets thrashed during vintage.

Any rules?
One cellar hand loves to sing really badly and loudly, so the only rule during vintage is to turn the stereo up loud enough so we can't hear him singing!

What's one interesting fact about you most people wouldn't know?
One thing that most people here wouldn't know would be that I used to be the lead singer in a band (laughs) - it was called Dazed and Confused and we just did rock covers. You could say that it described us too. I was just the singer.

Did you look the same in your DC days?
No, I had much longer hair… well, hair!

What would you do if you weren't a winemaker?
I'd probably be a chef or a bad musician!

What's the strangest job you've ever had apart from winemaking?
Making plastic bags in a factory - it was a stopgap in between some travel and starting university and I needed a job and got a job in a plastic bag factory making plastic bags for six months - it was terrible. You stick big rolls of plastic down a machine that makes all sorts of noises and goes up and down and spits out plastic bags at the other end.

wine

There've been some good years at Church Road recently, though Chris modestly demurs that it's not just because he's been winemaker - "the vintages have been fantastic!"

The Church Road Merlot Cabernet is a full-bodied, complex blend of Merlot, Cabernet Sauvignon and Malbec, whose dark berry aromas are complemented by complexities of liquorice and spice. It's a dry red with concentrated flavours and ripe tannins (the wine term for slightly bitter acids) with a long finish. With careful cellaring, it will reward you with more complex flavours and aromas.

Chardonnay's one of Chris' favourite wine styles, and the powerful and elegant Church Road Reserve Hawke's Bay Chardonnay is one of his best. Made from hand-picked grapes and with traditional winemaking techniques to add extra complexity, a richer mouth-feel and a softer palate. With concentrated, complex ripe peach and citrus flavours complemented by toasty oak undertones, it's balanced with gentle acidity to produce a bouquet of complex flavours and textures which will become even more integrated over five years.

The Cuve (pronounced Koov) Series is Chris' pride and joy. An exclusive, small-batch series released primarily through the cellar door, the Cuve Series Syrah is grown exclusively on the reddish, low vigour soils of Church Road's Redstone Vineyard in the Ngatarawa Triangle district and hand-picked before being fermented in French oak cuves (hence the name!). A supple, medium-bodied red full of fragrant fruit and gamey complexity, it's a brilliant match to rich, game and meat dishes.

vineyard

One of New Zealand's oldest working wineries, Church Road is set on an idyllic 1.5 hectare park, fringed by native gardens and a Merlot vineyard. As well as the winery (where you might catch Chris at work) and the Cuve cellar where the reds are fermented, you'll also find the famous Tom McDonald Cellar (built as a tribute to the father of New Zealand prestige reds), the fascinating Wine Museum (which includes the oldest winemaking relics in the country, dating back to the Iron Age)... and two petanque courts which always prove popular!

Church Road's renowned chef Malcolm Redmond serves some of Hawke Bay's best food in a charmingly rustic setting - with catering for private functions of up to 120 diners in the magical, sparkling atmosphere of the cellar, shimmering with gem-like tartaric crystals, vestiges of all the wine made there.

For only $NZ 10, you can enjoy a guided winery and museum tour, with a tasting included, with opportunity to purchase some rare vintages, such as the exclusive Cuve series.

Church Road Winery
50 Church Road, Taradale, Hawke's Bay
ph [64 6] 844 2053
info@churchroad.co.nz   www.churchroad.co.nz/
Cellar Door: 9am - 5pm everyday
Wine tastings, including a winery tour, cost $NZ 10 per person
Winery tours take place at 10am, 11am, 2pm and 3pm daily

kim crawford wines

kim crawford wines

erica and kim crawford - principals and winemakers

Meeting one day a the top of Table Mountain during South Africa's first nouveau wine festival, it wasn't exactly love at first sight for Kim and Erica Crawford. Well, not for Erica, anyway, whose heart didn't skip a beat. "I saw this bloke and thought 'Ugh, God, not my type at all!' But when I asked him his name and he replied 'Kum', I thought 'Wow! That's exotic! I wonder what kind of name that is?' When I asked him to spell it, he said 'K-I-M' and I tried not to look too disappointed… My first brush with the Kiwi accent - and of course, not the last!"

Luckily for the affable and laconic Kim - and for New Zealand winemaking - it didn't end there. Erica eventually left her job as a medical scientist ("I researched the genesis of cardiac arrhythmias in dogs, rats and baboons") and her home country to join Kim in New Zealand. Over a glass of wine in London, Kim and Erica decided with youthful exuberance and "self-righteousness" they could make better wine than they were drinking, and in 1996, they founded one of New Zealand's first "virtual wineries": with grapes sourced from growers, wine made at other wineries, and sold from their central Auckland home. With no estate to name it after, they simply called it Kim Crawford Wines, which, unlike their maker, are definitely easier to love at once!

Would you encourage your kids into winemaking?
Erica: Yes! They do their little stints in the winery. Rory, who's 13, has a really good palate and he's really interested in cooking. Pia, who's 12, has a great nose but I'm not sure what she's going to do.
Kim: Well, it's an nice job: you get to travel the world, especially when you're younger.

Is there a major goal you'd like to achieve before you stop stomping grapes?
Erica: My next project is to plant a little block we have in the … with funky little varietals.
Kim: It'd be nice to something a little more… eclectic, where you don't have to worry about the money, or deal with brand screwers around the world.

Corks vs screw tops?
Erica: We were the first Kiwi winery to do it! From a scientific perspective, we did it totally for wine quality reasons - wine can show flaws so quickly. I'm not saying it's the best stopper ever but at this time, it's the best we can do for our wine.
Kim: I'd agree. It suits our wine styles pretty well and keeps them really fresh and fruity, which is what we're all about.

What's your favourite drinking game?
Erica: I don't do those anymore! I'm a mum!
Kim: I can't remember what it's called, but it's the one where you put your finger on the glass and you have to guess how many fingers are on the glass, then drink it….

What's the best glass of wine you've had?
Erica: It'd have been at wine dinner presented by Krug and they had a chardonnay that was absolutely stunning.
Kim: Most probably a Mouton Rothschild '61, my birth year - it's not often that you get wines in this country of that age that have held together that well. I hope I have too!

What do you drink apart from wine?
Erica: Water and green tea at the moment. I'm trying to detox. It's hard in a winery!
Kim: Beer at harvest like every other winemaker.

How do you deal with wine tossers?
Erica: Disdainfully!
Kim: I don't mind them because at least they're interested in wine. It's some people in the industry who have an overstated opinion of themselves that I find more irritating.

erica & kim crawford

Best wine tosser story?
Erica: There are loads! Like the time a guy in America asked in all seriousness how we got the wood out of unwooded chardonnay...

What's the strangest job you've ever had apart from winemaking?
Erica: One uni holiday I was a nurse's aide at a mental hospital. That was a strange job! There was one old lady called Queenie who used to wear this terrible perfume I'll never forget. She was always made up to the tee - and she loved sex. She pestered all the male patients for sex.

If you could swap jobs with anyone for a week, who would it be?
Erica: I'd like to have a go at being a really good journalist, somewhere like the New Yorker magazine.
Kim: A farmer again I suppose - probably a dry stock farmer. But I'd have to find a farm in the city so my wife'd keep living with me!

What would you like to do before you go to the great vineyard in the sky?
Erica: I have a lot of schemes, but this year I really want to do a bungy jump. There are books I want to read and people I want to see. The one thing I'm really excited about is that little block I mentioned before, I can't wait to plant that.
Kim: One of my focuses is spending time with the kids as they go through their teenage years and to make wines that people really remember. Or failing that, make a wine Erica likes enough to let me name after her!

wine
As the old saying goes, "good things come in small parcels" and it's especially true of high-quality wine. Every vintage, Kim keeps a special batch of exceptional grapes from particular vineyards to make his premium Small Parcel SP series.

The Mistress SP Waipara Riesling is so called because it's grown on the site of the former estate of a wealthy Waipara landowner, who, on his regular trips to Christchurch, used to pop into his mistress's place on the way there and back! You can imagine how he might've bought her a bijou as a sign of his affection, perhaps? Kim Crawford's Mistress is similarly bejewelled, winning the Gold Medal at the New Zealand International Wine Show and Four Stars in the prestigious Decanter Magazine. With a typically Riesling bouquet of citrus, Granny Smith apples and honey, it tastes of citrus zest, apricot and a hint of honey. Intense and full-bodied, it's a great dry aperitif or accompaniment to Asian dishes or delicate white meats.

The SP Spit Fire Marlborough Sauvignon Blanc takes its name from the Delta vineyard, which was once used as an air force base during World War II. Like its aviationary counterparts, it's a winner, taking Gold at both the New Zealand International Wine Show

and the Air New Zealand Wine Awards. Hugely, intensely aromatic with nettle, grapefruit and tropical notes, it's a powerful, challenging wine with the herbaceousness typical of a great Marlborough Sauvignon Blanc, with inherently sweetish tropical fruit flavours balanced by dry herbs, gooseberry and tropical fruits. The full bodied flavours have a long-lasting finish and Erica loves it with oysters and lemongrass based dishes.

Hand-crafted with exceptionally small and concentrated fruit from the Comely Bank the brilliantly deep, almost black SP Comely Bank Marlborough Pinot Noir, whose elegant, restrained bouquet is redolent with red fruits, cherries and black plums, underscored with hints of toasty oak. With exceptional, juicy red and black fruit flavours, it should develop even more complexity with three to four years of careful cellaring, though it's great now with smoked salmon or lamb.

vineyard

As well as the wonderful, modern new winery, where you can taste and purchase Kim's prize-winning wines, there's also a fully self-contained one-bedroom apartment above the cellar door, the delightful Te Awanga Vineyard Lodge, designed with Erica's impeccable style. Stay for the weekend and see the sun come up over the vineyard in the morning, and the moon rising over the sea at night. The perfect escape…

Kim Crawford Wines
Clifton Road, Te Awanga RD2, Hastings
ph: [64 9] 309 1960
info@kimcrawfordwines.co.nz   www.kimcrawfordwines.co.nz

Cellar Door: Open for tastings, sales and picnics 11am to 5pm Saturday to Monday.
ph: [64 6] 875 0553 (phone first to check extra opening times)
christine@kimcrawfordwines.co.nz

stonecroft wines

stonecroft wines

alan limmer - founder and winemaker

After a series of "undrinkable fermentation experiments" while he was at school, and graduating with a Doctorate in Earth Sciences and Chemistry, Alan Limmer found himself in Hawke's Bay managing an analytical chemistry facility with links to the fledgling wine industry. It wasn't long before he wanted to make wine too - which led to seven long years without a holiday - and including the odd cyclone! - working at the lab during the day and planting and building the winery at night.

The gravely land around Stonecroft was considered up until the early 90s as a completely unarable wasteland, and over the years, Stonecroft's had a gravel quarry, an army firing range, a go kart track and a drag racing strip.

Not that that bothers Alan too much. A thrill-seeker from way back, he was an avid hang-glider before getting into karting with his son Kerryn (who also works at the vineyard) before progressing to the thirsty old "Beast" you can see in the picture. Although he confessed to his patient wife Glen only after she found out he'd bought two karts, she's now one of his biggest fans - "but only when I'm winning!" he says with a laconic laugh.

What makes a good winemaker?
You need attention to detail and a deep passion for it. The job's demands are more than just filling in a timesheet and rocking up. You need to be obsessed by it!

What's one of the hardest things about being a winemaker?
Trying to live with the mistakes! You're always trying to do something perfectly all the time and you rarely get there. Every year you think you'll have another crack at it, but no year's the same, so you always seem to be not quite where you want to be…

What's the worst disaster at vintage?
Picking during a cyclone - that wasn't much fun! They were trying to evacuate everyone but we had to pick the fruit. It was pissing down non-stop! We just kept going like drowned rats…

Best bit of advice you've been given in your career?
Focus on the fruit and the vineyard. Most people accept that now but I think 25 years ago most people tried to make it in the winery.

Art vs science in winemaking - your thoughts?
It's definitely a combination of both. You can't prescribe good wine simply with numbers because it defies those things. On the other hand it's not all black magic and voodoo either - you definitely need to borrow from both.

Are your kids interested in the business?
I suppose so - one drinks a lot and the other works in the vineyard!

How did you get into racing?
I'd always been a petrolhead but never had the money for it. Then one day, a mate came over and said he had a go kart, and did I want a go? I said no because I thought they were just kids' toys, but he convinced me to have a go and that was it. I bought one but didn't tell the wife - I used to keep it at his place and sneak off in the arvo to the track. Then my son Kerryn caught me at it, and I thought "Shit, I'll have to buy him one too now!" So I did and kept it at my mate's house too. Eventually I told the wife. Telling her about the Porsche I "forgot" to tell her about was another thing altogether…

What's your party trick?
Staying out of trouble… or trying to!

How do people react when you tell them you're a winemaker at dinner?
They seem to think it's terribly romantic, so I tell them to come and do a vintage and find out!

Who would you most like to share a glass of wine with?
Pass. If I told you I'd have to kill my wife!

What do you do to relax?
By getting away from the place by going fishing or racing. I used to go hang-gliding - until I got a winery!

Camping up the river with a few good mates and a few good bottles of wine is great too. Drinking a great wine out of a plastic cup while a freshly-snagged trout cooks on the fire - is there anything better than that?

What's your favourite getaway?
There's a lake about three hours' north that's just wilderness and bush. No mobiles or hotels or tourists: bloody brilliant.

What's it called?
I couldn't tell you that, or else I'd have to kill you!

What would you do if you weren't a winemaker?
I suppose I'd have to buy a lot of wine! But I'd love to be a race driver - Holden V8 Supercars'd do!

What would you like to do before you go to the great vineyard in the sky?
Um, catch more fish?

What would your last meal be - and what wine would go with it?
I'd love a feast of freshly-cooked crayfish and a good Chardonnay. Smoked trout's wonderful too. Sprinkle the fish with lots of brown sugar and salt, then let it sit for 24 hours. Drain it off, put it over manuka or tea tree sawdust in the smoker for 20 minutes, and eat it while it's still warm. Beautiful!

What's distinctive about your label?
Because the wines express who we are, what we are, the seasons that we've had: each year that's our life story in the bottle...

wine
Gewürztraminer, Chardonnay and Syrah are Alan's favourite varietals.

"I love Gewürz because it lends itself to a wide range of wine styles from sweet to dry; it's got so much character and it's so versatile. Having said that, it's a very hard grape to make any money out of it, so you really have to love it." And it wouldn't be hard to love Stonecroft's Old Vine Gewürztraminer, specially selected from Alan's originally-planted old vines, among the oldest in Hawke's Bay. A lovely pale green-gold, with a delicately perfumed bouquet with hints of lychee, it's lively and fresh with ginger and spice notes and hints of Turkish delight. Mmmm! With a long, spicy finish, it makes for great drinking now, though it should age extremely well.

Alan loves "freshly-snagged trout on the fire with a plastic cup of good Chardonnay," although you might want the good glasses for the Old Vine Chardonnay. Redolent of bread, toast and nuts, the palate has hints of white peach and hazelnuts, with a long citrussy, mineral tone that finally passes into a fine spicy acidity. Reflecting his love of Burgundian styles, Alan reckons this one'll "go the distance."

"Syrah's my absolute favourite," he says. "I love the texture and aromatics of it." Dark crimson and bursting with beautiful berry and floral fragrances, Stonecroft's Syrah is dominated by sweet cherry and black plum notes with a finely textured spicy finish.

vineyard

All Stonecroft's grapes are from their Mere Road and Tokarahi Vineyards, in the magical stony, free-draining soil of Hawke's Bay's best viticultural site, the Gimblett Gravels. Alan spent ages finding exactly the right sites and developing the vineyards to produce the best quality fruit, and even more time ensuring that the wines they produced are even better.

Although "we open our cellar door erratically and sometimes don't bother over winter" drop by Stonecroft and say hello to Alan and Glen at the cellar door. Well, Glen anyway - "she's the main cellar door attraction," says Alan. "She's much prettier and nicer than me and anyway, she doesn't let me loose on customers anymore!"

Give them a call to let them know you're coming - and to make sure they're open! But you can always purchase wine online securely and safely at Stonecroft's website.

Stonecroft Wines
RD 5, Mere Road, Hastings, Hawke's Bay
ph: [64 6] 879 9610
wine@stonecroft.co.nz   www.stonecroft.co.nz
Cellar Door: Open 11am - 5pm Saturday and 11am - 4pm Sundays
During the week between Christmas and New Year's - just call to confirm opening times.   Closed in winter.

corbans wines

corbans wines

tony robb - senior winemaker

Starting out in the IT industry, Tony Robb escaped to university to study psychology. Needing some extra funds to supplement his meagre student income, he got a job in a bottle shop, and encountered the infectious oenological enthusiasm of Martin Tillard (whom you may have already encountered in these pages). It wasn't long before he moved out of psychology too. He must've really loved winemaking, given that "there were three times as many women studying psychology as men - it was unreal for a young bloke," he says fondly. Especially given that most of the people he encounters at work are grizzled viticulturalists.

"I love the creative side of things," he says. And bike riding, at which he's especially accomplished. "I used to shave my legs every week, though I don't bother now - I realised I wasn't that good a cyclist to warrant doing it. That, and the snide comments I got in the vineyard…"

"I used to be pretty obsessive about my cycling," he recalls. "At one stage during my undergrad studies, I even sold my car, which forced me to cycle everywhere. I regretted it the first time I had to ride to the bottle store after a very unseasonal snow storm!"

Do you have nicknames in the vineyard?
Mine's Chog, short for Hedgehog, which refers to my hairstyle. But in general the vineyard managers refer to us as "bloody winemakers" which shows how annoying we can be. And we've been known to call them "gardeners"…

What annoys viticulturalists about winemakers, do you think?
I suppose because there tend to be more grey areas in winemaking than simply black and white and we have a tendency to always want to push it that little bit further. Well, I do! And at times, it can create a bit more work for the vineyard guys.

What makes a good winemaker?
You've got to have a good palate and you've got to be able to link that to your winemaking and have a good feel for what impact it has. For me, a wine's mouthfeel is just as important as its taste.

What do you like least about what you do?
Missing out on the best part of the fishing season!

How important are prizes?
Yes, I'd be lying if I said I didn't love seeing us get an award for something - whether it's a trophy or a medal or a great write up - but I'd hate to be forced into changing my philosophies in winemaking to get those accolades.

Is there a particular vintage experience you remember?
The one that really sticks is a practical joke we played on a guy years ago who used to make himself a little bath everyday in a big old barrel. We got sick of him taking the time off to do it so we half-filled the barrel with sugar, then poured hot water on top. For the next three days, he was a mild pink colour from a form of yeast infection. To this day he still doesn't know who did it (though I'm sure he will now if he reads the book)!

Do you talk much about wine at home?
Yeah, because my partner Katherine works in the industry as well. I actually met her when we both worked at Corbans nine years ago! Now she works for Esk Valley Winery in the cellar door and customer relations.

Do you/have you ever drunk cask wine?
I'll plead the 5th amendment on that one!

What music do you listen to at work?
Anything except country - we have a ban on "chicken kickin'" music. Although if someone brings along something rank it won't get a second glance.

Best wine tosser story?
I remember sitting alongside a prominent champagne maker once and quizzing him on how much influence over cork taint they had, and being told quite categorically that champagnes never suffer from cork taint while we drank a champagne he'd poured which was so spectacularly corked it wasn't funny. And then afterwards listening to him protest that it wasn't corked - "it was just terroir" - probably the most appalling use of the terroir concept (winespeak for the effect a vineyard's soil and micro-climate has on the wine) I've ever heard.

What's the strangest job you've ever had apart from winemaking?
Well, it wasn't the strangest but it was definitely the worst job I ever had. I used to work in a market garden and one of my jobs was looking after the battery hens we had. And that included going through the barn and killing all the ailing chickens. I've never eaten broilers or battery eggs since - only free-range. The whole issue of ethical farming production's something we all have to consider.

So do you follow ethical practices at Corbans?
Yeah, we're pretty much moving in that direction. We were one of the first wineries to be part of the Sustainable Wineries Program within Sustainable Winegrowing New Zealand which has the same environmentally-friendly philosophies applied to wine production as to grape growing. It's great to be a part of it, even if it means a bit more work.

wine

Corbans Private Bin is an exclusive series of premium hand-crafted wines made with grapes from a single region which exhibit all their varietals' - and regions' - classic characteristics and be ideal companions to good food. Hand-picking and whole-bunch pressing create a texturally elegant structure (winespeak for "a wine that feels good in the mouth") that accentuates winemaking subtleties.

The Corbans Private Bin Hawke's Bay Syrah is a complex wine whose peppery hints and savoury oak notes are tempered by its rich, fleshy sweet cherry and plum aromas. With its silky tannins and full-bodied finish, it's made for richly flavoured red meat dishes or game like duck and venison. While drinking well now, it'll continue to develop in complexity, peaking in a couple of years.

The Corbans Private Bin Hawke's Bay Chardonnay is a full and flavoursome example of the style. With lifted peach, nectarine and grapefruit notes, it's full of creamy texture, nutty complexity and lingering stonefruit and citrus flavours. It's the perfect accompaniment to a roast chicken salad served with a good Brie, a light vinaigrette - and perhaps some apricots! And it'll reward careful cellaring with even further depth over two to six years.

The wine Tony's most (rightly) proud of is the award winning Corbans Private Bin Hawke's Bay Gewürztraminer 2004 which added a Gold Medal to its groaning trophy cabinet at the Royal Easter Show in March last year, also winning Champion Gewürztraminer. Elegantly off-dry, it's redolent with rose petal aromas, complemented by subtle honeysuckle and hints of mandarin peel, balanced by a richly textured, oily palate with lingering musky rose flavours and appealing spicy ginger notes. It's great with lightly spiced South East Asian cuisine, especially duck or roast pork. It'll continue to evolve but because of its depth and complexity, it's best enjoyed within the next year or two.

vineyard

One of New Zealand's oldest wineries at over 100 years old, Corbans was founded in 1902 by a young Lebanese winemaker called Assid Corban. Initially selling wine from a truck that travelled the country, Corbans soon became one of New Zealand's finest wineries, long recognised for its contributions to the New Zealand wine industry, such as the first plantings of Chardonnay.

Today, Hawke's Bay is Corbans' heart: only the most exceptionally premium fruit from our Hawke's Bay vineyards is taken to Corbans' Winery in Napier to become the classic award-winning wine that bears the renowned Corbans Private Bin label.

Corbans Wines
91 Thames Street, Napier
ph: [64 9] 570 8445   NZ Freephone: 0800 736 611
info@corbans.co.nz   www.corbans.co.nz

seifried wines

seifried wines

chris seifried - winemaker

Winemaking's in Chris Seifried's DNA. "We have photos of us kids as babies - about six months or so - sleeping under the vines!" he says with a laugh. His father Hermann, originally from Austria, emigrated to New Zealand after studying winemaking in Germany and working in South Africa at what was then the world's largest winery, KWV. Meeting and marrying "true blue Kiwi girl" Agnes in 1971, with little more than a dream, he and his young bride purchased their first block of land to establish their vineyard - and start their family.

"At that stage there weren't a lot of tertiary-trained winemakers around," explains Chris. "The New Zealand industry was very small, and probably a bit parochial. When he first went to the bank with the idea that Nelson'd be a great place to grow wine, everyone thought he was mad. There was lots of tobacco and hops grown here at the time, but no grapes - everyone thought it was too cold."

Luckily, though, Hermann was persistent. From planting the first grapes in 1973, there are now 22 wineries in Nelson and Chris is "very proud of Dad for being a part of that."

Now, the whole family's involved, with elder sister Heidi helping with winemaking, younger sis Anna taking care of the marketing, Mum keeping admin in order, and Dad managing the vineyards, ensures Chris is never too snowed under...

How did you get into winemaking?
Mum and Dad were growing grapes before my two sisters and I were even born, so we obviously all grew up with wine all around us. I suppose it's always been in the family and something we were all just fell into. Growing up, all our spare time was helping in the vineyards driving tractors or helping picking grapes during harvest, or on the bottling line.

What does everyone do in the winery?
Mum looks after administration, finance and marketing. Dad looks after all the vineyards, the viticultural side, as well as overall management. My elder sister Heidi's a winemaker and dentist, and my younger sister Anna looks after the sales and marketing side of things.

Some say the winemaker's the one in control and the viticulturalist follows their lead. Is that what happens with you and your Dad?
Hell no! My old man's a big fellow in both stature and experience. He knows the winemaking game pretty well. He certainly does like to get involved in the winery and we do value his input and contributions. We all know how important it is that we all work together to make the best wines we can.

What's it like working with your Dad in that regard?
Well, being family, you know you can have it out with each other - expressing your opinions as forthrightly as you like! - and know you're not going to get fired in the morning. We're pretty lucky - we're completely family-owned so we're very relaxed around each other. It's important to know our opinions and ideas will be listened to - although maybe not always agreed with!

Do you have any other interests apart from winemaking?
I love skiing anytime of the year - snow skiing in winter and water skiing in summer. Of course, being Kiwi, I always enjoy a good game of rugby, but skiiing's my main sideline.

Have you skied in Austria?
When I was a very little fella of three or four, we went to Austria for Christmas, so I can't really remember getting on the runs! The most we did was toboggan down the driveway of my uncle's apple orchard.

chris seifried

Are you a good skier?
Well, I haven't done as much recently as I'd've liked to. I used to race a bit over the years, so I guess you could say I can hold my own.

Any good skiing stories?
Hey, what happens on tour stays on tour! But I've been lucky not to break any bones. Yet. Touch wood!

Best wine tosser story?
Hmmm, how do you choose? I have plenty! I don't spend a lot of time at the cellar door anymore but a few years ago, I was down there and this young couple came in. He obviously thought he knew a shitload about wine and was trying to impress her. As they worked through the wines they were tasting, it was pretty clear he was hip to doing all the talking and share his knowledge of wine with his lady. I didn't have to say anything! "Cabernet Merlot's a blend of Cabernet and Merlot," he said, which is of course correct. A few glasses later, I poured a Cabernet Sauvignon, which he duly explained was "a blend of Cabernet and Sauvignon Blanc." I had to bite my tongue - you do hear a lot of interesting comments at the cellar door!

Who is the biggest influence on you as a winemaker?
My Dad! He's done pretty damn good in my book: he started with nothing. Just to settle in a new country when you don't speak the language is pretty brave, but he went against the grain and did his own thing and did really well. I really respect what he's done.

Best bit of advice you've been given in your career?
Bob Cartwright, the renowned winemaker at Leeuwin Estate in Margaret River, whom I did a vintage with fresh out of uni, always used to say "if you're not at work at five to eight in the morning, then don't bother turning up, 'cos if you're not at work by 8am, then you've pissed me off so much I don't want to see you for the rest of the day." Winemaking-wise, Dad's always offering good bits of advice - some of which I listen to, and some I possibly don't!

wine

Reflecting its Austrian heritage and Nelson setting, Seifried's wines are perfect examples of the Austrian winemaking styles and New Zealand winemaking techniques.

The much lauded Seifried Sauvignon Blanc is fresh, lively, and bursting with flavour. It's picked from the Cornfield Vineyard adjacent to the winery - an ancient Maori kumara (sweet potato) bed which was spread by those ancient warriors with fine gravel and sand to provide suitable soil for their kumara plantings. With an intensely "savvy" nose that speaks straight from the vineyard, redolent of tropical passionfruit and pineapple, its citrussy acidity leads to a long, slightly mineraly finish. Yum! Ideal with scallops or a creamy pasta.

One of Seifried's best-known wines is Seifried Gewürztraminer - this is one many Kiwis have come to know and love over the years, winning numerous awards and acclaim. This wine's primarily grown on the unirrigated Redwood Valley vineyard. As a result, the already small-bunched grapes are even more concentrated and aromatic, with intense lychee and apricot aromas and a rich, powerful texture with a spicy, luscious, long finish. "It's a very intense wine," says Chris, "so match it with something with loads of flavour, like a spicy Thai curry with coriander."

Seifried's Winemaker's Collection is an exclusively selected and hand-crafted range of super-premium wines, of which the Nelson Riesling Ice Wine is a superb example. Made with only the finest Riesling grapes, hand-selected at the peak of ripeness and then pressed frozen to release very concentrated, intensely flavoured juice, this extraordinary wine bursts with intense luscious citrus and blossom aromas - "just like walking through an orchard in full spring bloom!" Chris reckons. With a powerful and concentrated palate, it's nevertheless well-tailored with a zippy acidic twist to temper the exceptional sweetness. Although it's enjoyable on its own, Chris thinks its lively layers of fruit and acidity would complement something refreshingly sweet like a mango sorbet or fresh fruit salad.

cellar door

Just ten minutes' drive from Richmond and twenty minutes' from the centre of Nelson, Seifrieds Vineyard Restaurant is a dining experience worth enjoying. What could be better than sipping on a glass of exquisite Seifried wine while sampling the culinary delights prepared by head chef René and his team, created to perfectly match the Seifried range? With an open fireplace during winter and the peaceful surroundings of the vineyard garden in summer, it's a wonderful place to relax or celebrate.

And of course, don't forget to purchase all your wine and wine-related accessories and souvenirs at the cellar door shop at the Rabbit Island Vineyard, close to the winery. The friendly and knowledgeable staff love answering questions about Seifried wines and any curlies you might have about viticulture or the vineyards.

Seifried Winery and Restaurant
Corner of State Highway 60 and Redwood Road (at the Rabbit Island Turnoff), Appleby, Nelson
ph: [64 3] 544 1555
wines@seifried.co.nz   restaurant@seifried.co.nz   www.seifried.co.nz
Cellar Door: Open Daily from 10am to 5pm

jules taylor wines

jules taylor wines

jules taylor - winemaker

A Marlborough girl, born and bred, Jules has wine flowing through her veins. Although she started out as a zoologist and says she ended up in winemaking "because I didn't want to finish uni", she's worked in a wide range of countries and wine regions, perfecting her craft, including eight vintages in Italy, along with stints at Yarra Ridge in Victoria and the Hunter Valley's famed Rothbury Estate. Since returning to New Zealand, she's worked at Villa Maria in Marlborough and successive vintages at Cloudy Bay. One of the few women working as a senior winemaker, she's cited as an influence by a new generation of New Zealand winemakers, who appreciate her expertise, her passion - and her sense of humour, which she somehow manages to keep in between her "day job" as winemaker at another major winery, moonlighting with her own wines, and looking after her two young sons Louis and Nico.

What do you love best about what you do?
That I don't have to wear ironed clothes to work!

What do you like least?
The Delhi Belly I get when we're tasting grapes in the vineyard at the start of harvest - too much acid (laughs)

What's one of the hardest things about being a winemaker?
Probably the hibernation from society during vintage - when you're working 24/7 and just going mad for six weeks, you don't get to really see your family and friends, and that sucks.

What's the worst wine "faux pas" you've ever made?
Touch wood I haven't made a major - but then, you know, vintage is coming up!

What's the worst disaster at vintage?
Running out of beer or coffee!

What challenges have you faced as a female winemaker in a very male dominated industry?
It was really only early on that things were difficult - getting my first job was really tough - the guy interviewing me at the time would say things like "Ooh, you know there'll be smelly men in the winery" and "you know you'll have to go up a ladder" and stuff like that - you know, just because it hadn't happened in his winery before - so once you get over those hurdles, nothing's really that difficult or different.

Is there a major goal you'd like to achieve before you stop stomping grapes?
I'd like to make some money for all my efforts (laughs)!

Best bit of advice you've been given in your career?
To go hard while your tyres are tight - basically, while you're still young and you've got the energy and stuff - you don't get those years back, so just go hard while you can.

Are you still going hard?
Shit yeah!

Worst bit of advice you've been given in your career?
That girls can't drive forklifts.

Did you show them a thing or two and prove 'em wrong?
Oh, shit yeah!

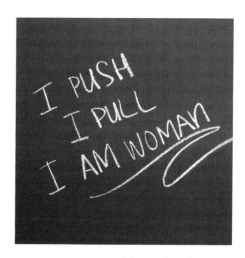

jules taylor, louis and nico

What's your favourite hangover cure?
Nurofen and coffee and hot croissants and bed!

What happens when you get a midweek hangover? Do you still stay in bed?
I used to say you have to go to work, until this last harvest party when I couldn't even get out from under the covers, but I'd say, yes, 99.9% of the time, I get up.

Do you have kids?
Yes, Louis (3) and Nico (18 months)

Do they want to be winemakers too?
Oh no - Louis wants to be a fireman, and Nico can't talk yet so I'm not sure where he's heading!

What's the strangest job you've ever had apart from winemaking?
De-tasselling corn over the summer when I was at high school…

How do you de-tassel corn?
You know the fluffy bit that sticks out of the top? Actually, you don't see those when you buy a corn cob at the supermarket - when corn grows, the tassel comes out the top, and it has the pollen stuff on it and if you're cross-pollinating two different varieties, you take all the tassels out of one lot and pollinate it with the other ones planted sort of interspersed in different rows… it's really really boring!

wine

Although her "little winemaking venture" has only been going for a few years, it comes with all of Jules' long experience in the industry. Sourcing her grapes from exclusive, "hands on" vineyards in Marlborough - and sometimes family friends! - Jules reckons that, whatever of her wines you choose, they're always best when enjoyed with great food and good friends!

Grown by old family friends, the Inders, on their vineyard in Grovetown, Jules' Chardonnay is hand harvested, the juice lightly settled before fermentation in a mix of old and new French oak barriques (which are large casks). With sweet, spicy oak and ripe stone fruit aromas, it has a rich complex palate with a long, full finish, which will evolve even further over three years from bottling.

Always released in limited quantities, Jules' Pinot Gris is sourced from the Wairau Valley on the north side of Marlborough and the Awatere Valley on the south to produce a luscious wine with both ripe flavours and complex structure. With a bouquet of sweet quince and nashi pears, this wine exhibits good weight and a finely textured palate.

"Now, I reckon the best thing to enjoy with my Pinot is my famous lemon cake, which Louis loves helping me make!" says Jules. Take 2 small cups of sugar, a cup of natural yogurt, 2 eggs, a cup of canola oil, a cup of thread coconut, 2 cups of self raising flour, the zest of 4 lemons and the juice of one lemon. Mix the everything but the flour and coconut in a large bowl, and then fold the flour and coconut once it's nice and mixed. Bake at 180°C for an hour, and while it's baking, make a syrup of lemon juice and caster sugar. After turning the cake out, pour the sugar over, and scoff with Jules' Pinot Gris and natural yoghurt. "Or if you're feeling piggy, whipped cream," adds Jules.

This is the third year for Jules' Sauvignon Blanc, and "preferring to let the fruit do the talking", she blended grapes from three distinct areas in Marlborough to encourage punchy aromatics, ripe mid-palate flavours and a long finish. Redolent of freshly cut capsicum, passionfruit and white currant, the "Savvy" (as she likes to call it) has a mouth filling, dry finish, making it a distinct example of Marlborough's signature wine, which she reckons is always good with green-lipped mussels with a spicy puttanesca sauce on pasta.

vineyard
Although she sources her grapes from the very best growers, Jules doesn't have her own vineyard… yet! But you can buy her wines from any good premium wine retailer, or find them and buy them online at Hancock's (one of New Zealand's biggest and best premium wine distributors).

Jules Taylor Wines
P O Box 897, Blenheim, Marlborough
ph: [64 3] 578 3190
jules@julestaylor.com   www.julestaylor.com

te whare ra

te whare ra

jason and anna flowerday - proprietors and winemakers

Marlborough's oldest boutique winery, Te Whare Ra nonetheless has an exuberant sense of youth in the vineyard nowadays. Since taking over in 2003, Jason and Anna Flowerday have brought a breath of fresh air to a winery that had seen better days, not only taking over the 28 year old Gewürztraminer vines, but replanting sections of the vineyard with Syrah, Pinot Gris, Sauvignon Blanc and more Riesling.

They both have wine in their blood, having grown up in wine country - Jason a Marlborough boy through and through; and Anna, a McLaren Vale gal, being the fifth generation of a wine-growing family, who ended up becoming assistant winemaker at the prestigious Tintara Winery there, where she met Jason in 1999.

After working in the Clare Valley together, they decided on settling down in a place of their own. Twin daughters Sophie and Emily soon followed. "It was a dream come true for us," says Anna. "We're living the dream," adds Jason. And it's being added to by another set of twins soon!

For the Flowerdays, "boutique" doesn't mean "small" but "handcrafted": "It's more a way of doing things than size," says Jason. Centred on premium, small-batch, hand-picked, hand-crafted estate-grown wines, their perfectionist attitude to making wine stands in contrast to their relaxed attitude to drinking it. "It is just fermented grape juice, after all," says Anna with a laugh. "We make wine we like drinking ourselves," adds Jason. "If it doesn't sell, at least we can drink it!"

How do you make wine together?
Anna: Luckily we have pretty similar thoughts about winemaking and we agree about 90% of the time - the remaining 10% makes it interesting, though we've had some heated discussions! I suppose if we agreed any less, we'd probably get nothing done, and we'd've broken up by now! We had worked together before we started the winery together, so I guess we knew we were hopefully going to get through vintage without killing each other!
Jason: It's an equal sort of thing. We bring our own individual skills to each style we make - Anna's good at some things and I'm good at others.

Is it hard making wine with your spouse?
Jason: No, we work really well together - we have similar passions and agree on most things. She's taught me a lot and we've learnt a lot from each other. She's my best friend.
Anna: It definitely has its moments, though!

What are some of the challenges you've faced in such a male-dominated industry, Anna?
Anna: Well, it's changed a lot. Some pioneers, like Pam Dunsford at Chapel Hill (in McLaren Vale, South Australia) were the first, so they had it a lot tougher than I did - a third of my year at uni were chicks. It's probably a bigger issue for women working for the bigger companies, especially when it comes to maternity leave and stuff like that - they're not really used to dealing with that. But otherwise, it's pretty accepted now, and it's a lot easier when you're the co-owner!

What was it like doing vintage when you were pregnant?
Anna: I was lucky enough to do it when I was still in the early stages, so I wasn't too uncomfortable. But I was mindful of the fact that I couldn't sit down at the end of the day with a G n' T or a beer - my mum joked that I was probably the soberest since I was 16!

Would you encourage your girls to be winemakers too?
Anna: Well, we'd love it if they wanted to, but we won't be heartbroken if they didn't

sophie, jason, anna and emily flowerday

either. But hopefully they will! Sophie'll be good at PR but Emily's a bit more tomboyish and more interested in food so she'll probably be the one who makes the wine.

Jason: I reckon they already are! Sophie says her favourite is Peeno and Emily's is Savvy!

Why did you start your winery in Marlborough rather than McLaren Vale?

Anna: The opportunity came up and it was too good an opportunity here to say no to. Although we wanted to move back near either family - whether McLaren Vale or here - we noticed how belts in Australia had tightened, while New Zealand's still in a bit of a boom phase.

Jason: They're both beautiful regions and make truly great wines. But Marlborough offered us the best opportunity at the time - where else could we have bought a winery and vineyard with the reputation and history ours has?

What's distinctive about your label?

Anna: Well, we designed the actual label itself, so we love it - I think it's elegant and classic. The winery's the oldest boutique winery in Marlborough - we've got the oldest vines. And Te Whare Ra's always been known as something unique: unlike Sauvignon Blanc, which is Marlborough's signature grape, our flagship varieties are Gewürz and Riesling - so whenever anyone's looking for something a little bit different, we've got something for them.

Jason: Absolutely - couldn't have put it better myself! All our wines comes from our own little vineyard, they're all hand-made on site in small, limited release batches - and we do everything here ourselves. We only release our best wines and don't compromise on anything!

wine

"We want wine to be fun!" chime Anna and Jason. "In, say, Mediterranean cultures, the wine in the glass isn't as paramount as the food on the table and the people sitting at it with you - that doesn't mean we don't want to make great wine, but we do want people to taste some of the passion we feel, doing something we love."

And you can certainly taste it, in exceptional wines hand-crafted from Marlborough's oldest vines. Reflecting both Flowerdays' love of aromatic whites, their much-lauded Riesling and Gewürztraminer are both intensely pure expressions of those old vines.

With lifted white floral aromas, Kaffir lime leaves, fresh lemon and bath-salts and a finely structured palate bursting with vibrant fresh lime, lemon sorbet and ripe grapefruit, the hand-picked Riesling is balanced by a lingering minerality that provides a long, lingering, dryish finish, which makes it ideal with scallops, whitebait or King George whiting. Although enjoyable to drink now, it'll benefit from careful cellaring for six to eight years.

"I love Pinot because it's a challenge," says Anna, "and when you get it just right…" Judges and drinkers agree, with TWR Pinot Noir having been lauded for its bright fragrant aromas of ripe strawberry, black cherry and hints of mocha, violets and spice, its finely textured, silky tannins swirl around vibrant cherry and plum flavours, balanced by subtly savoury finish which is nonetheless infused with lingering fruit and well-integrated oak that makes it ideal with any rich duck dish or Anna's famous mushroom risotto.

The TWR Gewürz is a typically intensely perfumed example of the style, with notes of rose-petals, ripe quince, lychees and cloves, which lead into luscious baked quince and lychee flavours, underpinned by fresh pears and hints of exotic ginger and spice. Hand-picked from Te Whare Ra's oldest vines, it's also good for drinking now, but will also benefit from six to eight years in the cellar. Its weight and spice make it a great match for Asian cuisine, roast pork or bouillabaisse.

vineyard

Te Whare Ra means "house in the sun" in Maori, and, as you sip a glass of wine while you watch the sun linger over the vineyards, you'll understand what it means.

With some of Marlborough's oldest vines, it's a lovely place, ringing with children's laughter. It's a winery, but it's also a home.

The tasting room's located upstairs in the quaint mud-brick winery. There's a bell at the top of the stairs: ring for Jason and Anna to come and show you round, and while you're waiting, why not take in the breathtaking views of the vineyards and the spectacular mountains of the Richmond Ranges surrounding the Wairau River plain?

Give Anna and Jason a call, and you may be able to catch one of their regular vineyard tours and regular seasonal activities such as barrel tastings. And the best part is that unlike many wineries, you'll be tasting wine poured by the people who actually made it!

Te Whare Ra
56 Anglesea Street, Renwick, Marlborough
ph: [64 3] 572 8581
tewharera@xtra.co.nz   www.te-whare-ra.co.nz
Tasting Room: Open Daily 11am - 5pm in Spring and Summer
Open by appointment in Winter

spy valley

DEFENCE AREA
NO ADMISSION EXCEPT ON BUSINESS
ANY PERSON PROCEEDING BEYOND THIS NOTICE
OR REMAINING IN THIS DEFENCE AREA IS
SUBJECT TO RESTRICTIONS IMPOSED UNDER
PART III OF THE DEFENCE REGULATIONS 1990
AND MAY AT THE DISCRETION OF THE

OR OF ANY AUTHORISED PERSON BE DETAINED
AND SEARCHED BOTH AS TO HIS OR HER PERSON,
AND AS TO ANY VEHICLE, SHIP, BOAT, AIRCRAFT,
RECEPTACLE, PARCEL, OR CHATTEL IN HIS OR
HER POSSESSION OR UNDER HIS OR HER CONTROL
by order of
MINISTER OF DEFENCE

spy valley

ant mackenzie - winemaker

Spy Valley is the colloquial name for Marlborough's Waihopai Valley, given the presence of those two big balls in the background there - a satellite communications monitoring base. Can't say what's in those balls, but there's definitely something in the water - or the grapes! - at Spy Valley, which, thanks to winemaker Ant Mackenzie, has been cleaning up critical acclaim and prizes in magazines and shows around the world.

Ant's start in the wine industry was cemented when the winemaker at the cellar door he was working at said "Well, we've been let down for vintage and we need somebody with an HT licence to drive the truck and take the skins away and if you're prepared to work night shift, we've got a job for you." Although he didn't have a licence, he borrowed the vineyard truck, loaded it up with bags of cement, drove it round town, got his licence - and his break!

After loads of travel, and working in wineries and wine regions around the world before returning to Marlborough eleven years ago, he worked at Framingham before coming to Spy Valley, where he's more than happy to share his experiences and ideas - "nothing's classified!"

What do you love best about what you do?
I'd have to say meeting people - it's one of those jobs where you get to travel quite a lot. It's a good career if, like me, you're an expert at nothing in particular. And what I really love is there's no particular rules: there's no right or wrong way to do things, and you can discover things along the way… most importantly, because I love eating, drinking and travelling, it's been a great career choice!

When's the best time?
I'd have to say bud burst, when all the grasses in the hills start to grow and you're just starting to see flecks of green on the vines. It's the prettiest time in the vineyard for me. From a work perspective, harvest's the best time, because you've got the satisfaction of having picked everything and all the work having been done (until you have to think about bottling it all!). And even then, it's still pretty lovely: you'll find yourself in the vineyard in the afternoon, seeing the vine leaves starting to yellow and redden. Beautiful.

What do you do to relax?
Right now I'm on a real gardening kick, and I've started a veggie garden with the usuals: lots of salad greens, rocket, tomatoes, a few spuds I haven't dug up yet, courgettes… we've dug up all our spinach and silverbeets, and I've got a bit of sweetcorn coming on.

Do you go to other vineyards or wine regions on your holidays?
Never! My wife and I are from Hawkes Bay, so we do spend a bit of time up there, but we never visit wineries there or anything, which is kind of ironic, but then it'd be a bit of a busman's holiday if you did that, wouldn't it?

Sideways - yay or nay
Nay (laughs)! It's too naff! I had to go see it though, to see what the fuss was all about. But then, the Napa Valley's a bit like Disneyland! I once did a six month oenology internship in a small town called Saint Helena in the Napa Valley and had an absolutely awesome time…

We often get people ringing up and saying "We love wine, can we come and work in the winery for free?" But we pretty much say no because it's that kind of industry where so many people are so interested and motivated who've gone out and worked and studied, that we don't need any sea-change lawyers in their mid-forties that want something romantic.

On the one hand, you feel bad about giving them jobs because the realities of winemaking mean that the entry level jobs in a winery are very un-romantic, to say the least, just like thinking you can cook and getting a job in a restaurant and having to peel the spuds - in a winery, it's cleaning the drains and water-blasting the floor…

Which five people would you have to your dream dinner party?
My granddad, who's dead; Ernest Hemingway, through my escapades in Spain, I reckon he'd be interesting; some of my mates from Lincoln University - a couple of classic classmates, also fellow winemakers; Owen Bird, a crazy Taswegian who married a German opera singer and makes wine in Europe now - he just wrote a great book on Riesling.

What would your last meal be - and what wine would go with it?
Scallops with a lime salsa, and getting down and dirty with crayfish, digging out the meat - cutting them in half, breaking off the legs, getting into the sauce from the stomach cavity, with a great bottle of Moselle-style Riesling.

wine

Growing eight varieties of grapes on 360 acres set on the sunny side of Marlborough's Wairau Valley, Spy Valley's wines are noted for their "youthful exuberance", bursting with intense fruit flavours and fragrant aromas, capturing the essence of their seasons and setting, as reflected in their immensely successful season this year, winning an astounding array of prizes and critical acclaim - with Spy Valley being the first winery in the Sydney International Wine Show's history to win four trophies!

Spy Valley's 2006 Riesling, which won the coveted Blue Gold and a place in the Top 100 and a trophy in the prestigious Sydney International Wine Competition, is a pale green beauty, with apple, lime and mineral aromas, and a hint of sweetish apricot and honey. With pure, clean flavours framed by acidity and balanced by fruit sweetness, it's perfect for easy drinking, or perhaps enjoyed with some seared scallops dressed with chilli, ginger and lime.

Spy Valley Gewürztraminer is a thrilling example of this fragrant, floral, rebellious style. With lifted aromas of rose petals and Turkish delight and undertones of cinnamon and coriander, which, given his love of Thai food, Ant reckons is "an awesome flavour - I often see it in Gewürz and when people talk about spiciness in Gewürz, I see that coriander note… and of course it's wicked with Thai food, when you load in the coriander at the end."But guess what Ant reckons it's the perfect match for? "A ham sandwich," he says. "Honestly!"

"Pinot's definitely the biggest challenge," Ant says, laughing. "And we've managed to chance some good ones!" And Spy Valley's Pinot Noir is one of the best. Winner of the Gold and Champions List at the New Zealand International Wine Show and snaring five stars in Restaurant Wine Magazine, this deep ruby-red, full-bodied, richly flavoured wine bursts with dark berry aromas and a lively

mix of intensely fruity blackcurrants, plums, chocolate and spice. With a touch of mild oakiness and a long finish, it's a great accompaniment to gamey dishes or, for something different, try it with smoked tomato and molasses glazed salmon...

vineyard

In addition to all those grapes, Spy Valley also boasts over two thousand olive trees thriving on ground considered too hard for grapes. "Apart from a more efficient use of the land, and providing a bit of shelter for native animals, the olive trees - and the oil and fruit they produce - really complement what we do: the olive harvest's after the grape harvest, and instead of giving people something cheesy like a corkscrew or hat, we give them a bottle of our hand-pressed olive oil, which they can enjoy with our wine, of course!"

If you're visiting Spy Valley and want to make a weekend of it, why not check out the Timara Lodge, adjoining the vineyard? Owned and operated by the Johnsons, who also run Spy Valley, it's one of New Zealand's most luxurious and private lodges, set on 600 magnificently sculptured acres, boasting a five-acre man-made lake and a restaurant boasting critically acclaimed cuisine by the internationally-renowned chef Louis Schindler (who'll also be your host during your stay), and designed to perfectly complement Spy Valley's award-winning wines. Use it as a base for your Marlborough explorations - if you can tear yourself away!

Spy Valley Wines
Johnson Estate Limited, RD6 Waihopai Valley Road, Marlborough
ph: [64 3] 572 9840
info@spyvalley.co.nz   www.spyvalley.co.nz
Cellar Door: Open Daily 10am - 4pm in Summer (mid Oct - end Apr)
Monday - Friday 10am - 4pm in Winter (1 May - mid Oct)
Timara Lodge
Dog Point Road, RD2 Marlborough
ph: [64 3] 572 8276
timaralodge@xtra.co.nz   www.timara.co.nz

framingham wine company

framingham wine company

andrew hedley - winemaker

Originally from Gateshead in the north of England, Andrew Hedley was offered the lab manager's job at Rapaura Vintners over the phone at very short notice - John Belsham, the owner, called him the day before Christmas Eve 1997, and he moved down under to start work on the 6th of January! Becoming Framingham's winemaker in 2002, his love of the new is reflected in his continual drive for innovation in Framingham's range of aromatic wines, trying new methods and varietals in ways that surprise, rather than shock - although you could say his family was a bit more than shocked when he moved across the world to pursue his dream.

"I'm not a big one for making plans and goals," he says. "If you do follow them slavishly, you could miss out on other opportunities, but I had half an idea that maybe I could become a winemaker in ten years." It only took him four - even if he's still trying to come to terms with New Zealand's favourite pastime (the non-ovine one).

Though his admittedly perfectionist approach to his job makes it hard for him to relax, he's hardly uptight about wine itself: 'I'm not really into the "wine with rules" thing,' he says. 'I believe people should drink whatever makes them happy.'

What music do you listen to at work?
I'm an ageing punk rocker these days, so I love all that kind of thing mostly from the seventies. Sex Pistols, Clash, Buzzcocks, Ramones, Undertones, Stiff Little Fingers… stuff like that.

Um, winemaking's not very punk, is it?
No, I suppose not! Someone once came up to me at a tasting and asked me how I could make wine and wear a Sex Pistols t-shirt? Of course I love the noise and colour of punk but most of all, I love its can-do, F-you attitude. I guess we try and take that DIY attitude when we're trying different things in the winery - you might end up with a new wine!

Having said that, while Framingham's wines are "my" wines in a sense, I make them for everyone to enjoy. So I can't go about being maverick with its reputation, heritage and customer base. Rather than going for punk's shocking newness, it's a question of evolution rather than an abrupt change.

Of course, over the years I've thought about my own label - idle doodles here and there - and although the wines mightn't be too much different, the imagery and packaging certainly would - I mean, nobody's doing anything like that and I've got a sneaky feeling it might have some appeal. But then again, if you want to make complex and interesting wine, you have to accept a certain kind of customer will buy it, and I just don't see snotty punk kids wanting to buy it. Then again, there are a lot of successful middle-aged punks out there…

What's one interesting or unusual fact about you many people wouldn't know?
My life would be seriously uninteresting to most people so there's not much! At the beginning of 2006, my larynx was removed due to cancer, which means I can't talk without an artificial aid.

How's your life changed as a result?
Well, I can't go swimming! When they remove your larynx, they separate your oesophagus (food pipe) and trachea (windpipe). My mouth and nose are still connected, but the main difference is that I don't breathe through my mouth or nose anymore, but a hole in my throat. Basically, my lungs'd fill up with water if I went swimming as they're essentially open to the atmosphere. So I don't do a lot of boating, kayaking or surfing either! And I can't stand directly under the shower.

I talk with the assistance of an electronic aid called a servox, which I hold against my neck. It's not so bad, and most people can understand me okay - and you adapt very

quickly anyway. Part of my job's talking and tasting with groups of people, and I've just gotten on with it, really. I do try and make a light-hearted comment early on to put people at ease, but I've found most people are genuinely nice and understanding.

One thing: the servox can get buzzy if the volume's up too loud, so I've got a head mike for tastings and presentations, and I look just like Madonna on stage. If the lighting's right, of course!

Did the laryngectomy affect your palate in any way?
I was shitting myself about that - obviously, not being able to breathe through my nose would mean I mightn't be able to smell anything. Not that I'd lose my sense of smell, but how would I get aromas up there? I've learnt - with no effort at all, really - a method called "the polite yawn", where you close your lips and expand your mouth cavity, rather like you would if you were politely stifling a yawn. When you do this, air has to be drawn in and the only way it can get in is through your nose! As long as I use a glass that tapers at the top, I find I can get enough aroma up my nose to smell quite happily. And my sense of taste wasn't affected in any way, thank goodness. I'm able to evaluate things in the same way I used to. A major relief!

Have you found anything good's come out of it?
I suppose there's always something good to take away from most things. I did get a lot of perspective - sure, I lost my larynx, but I also didn't lose my life, and the cancer's now gone, thank God. I guess I should have learnt to "smell the roses" more (yes, I know, bad choice of words!) but then again, unlike most people, I can choose when and what I smell - great if you're caught in a lift with someone farty!

And if I don't feel like talking to someone, I can pretend the old servox's run out of batteries!

Do you consider yourself a Kiwi now, or still English?
Well, all my family still live in Gateshead, and we try and visit as much as we can. Besides, I came after I was 30, so I was pretty well formed by then, and so I'd have to say I still very much consider myself English. That and the fact I fail the main criteria for being Kiwi: I hate rugby passionately. Bloody horrible game!

wine

The first wine made under the Framingham label, a Riesling, was released in 1994, and today, Framingham produces a range of varietals including Riesling, Sauvignon Blanc, Chardonnay, Pinot Gris, Gewürztraminer and Pinot Noir from some of Marlborough's oldest and best vineyards.

With a low harvest yield and late picking, Framingham's Marlborough Pinot Gris is a pale rose gold wonder, with generous "Apple Strudel" flavours of apple (obviously!), pear, raisins, cream and custard, resulting in a long, creamy finish. Yum! And while its rich fruit flavours are immediately appealing, its complexity will continue to develop and deepen over the next two to three years.

If Marlborough's famous for its aromatic wines, Framingham's rightly renowned for its much-awarded Classic Riesling, an intense yet delicate wine with rich citrus flavours and juicy acidity. It's got a lovely lifted bouquet of honeysuckle and apricots, with hints of white pepper and Kaffir lime - an already approachable young wine, Andrew reckons it has the potential to develop further in the bottle. Very versatile with food, it's great with scallops or other seafood, and exceptional with Chinese cuisine.

Although Framingham's core range is based around aromatic whites, it's complemented by other varieties such as Pinot Noir. Framingham's Pinot Noir is a great example of Andrew's commitment to excellence. An attractive bright garnet-coloured wine, with a pretty, berryish bouquet and juicy, sweet flavours of raspberry and cherry. With its concentrated texture and supple tannins (winespeak for the dryness in red wine), it's immediately approachable but should continue to soften and deepen over the next couple of years. It's a natural match for classic game and lamb dishes, but try it with red, meaty fish like tuna or salmon.

vineyard

Framingham gets its name from the village of Framingham in South Norfolk, England, the ancestral home of its founder, Rex Brooke-Taylor. Its vineyards date back to the early 80s when Rex started planting in relatively young, stony, free-draining riverbed soils just outside Renwick.

Visitors are welcome to taste and buy wine at the cellar door all year round. A charming haven of landscaped courtyard gardens planted with roses, "mop top" trees and native flora, Framingham's understandably become one of the "must see" attractions on the Marlborough wine trail, despite being such a small boutique winery.

The tasting room resonates an ambience of style and attention to detail, with a staircase leading to the underground cellars, where a blossoming museum of vintages past and present are kept, along with a trove of oenological memorabilia. Best of all, Andrew likes to release special, limited release wines such as Framingham Select Riesling through the cellar door, which aren't generally available anywhere else.

Framingham Wine Company Ltd
PO Box 37, Conders Bend Road, Renwick, Marlborough
ph: [64 3] 572 8884
info@framingham.co.nz   www.framingham.co.nz

clayridge vineyards

clayridge vineyards

mike just - winemaker

A direct descendant of the legendary King Edward III of England and his son, the Black Prince, Michael Edward Just is not "just" any winemaker. How many winemakers have a full suit of armour in the closet and are building a castle on their property?

A passion for family history - and home brewing! - led Mike to Germany, where he learnt German, winemaking, and the art of jousting. Medieval sword fighting and tournaments became a way of life - as well as learning how to tame the mercurial Pinot grape.

Having worked in a number of German wineries after finishing his training, Mike returned to New Zealand with his wife Paula, working at a number of wineries here, including Lawson's Dry Hills, where in his eight years there, his wines were awarded six trophies, 20 gold medals and achieved Top 100 status in America.

Despite his many interests, including building a castle and restoring his beloved '69 Monaro GTS, Mike also manages to fit in winemaking duties not just for Clayridge, but three other wineries! However, his first love is Clayridge, and it's reflected in the "individual" wines he makes, which like him, all have their own very individual personality.

What's distinctive about your label?
I make wines with personality. I think it's important not to seek perfection, like you might airbrush a picture. I like wines with interesting traits. I'm always striving to achieve a bit more than just the varietal characteristics: I like to weave in as much complexity as I can. All my wines have some degree of wild barrel ferment in them - they're wines with a bit of individuality and personality.

Why don't you use irrigation?
When we found the perfect site for our vineyard back in 1999, it was up a dirt road in the middle of a paddock with no ready water source. I'd worked with non-irrigated vines before - mainly in Europe - and I really liked the small berries and balance those vines had achieved. The key thing about small berries for Pinot Noir means the wine achieves better colour, better tannins, and better flavour structure. Where other people have had to spray their vineyards four or five times, we've only sprayed ours once. But more importantly, practically, it means that, should my son or his son follow me in the family business, they'll still be able to make wine off the same vineyard, without plundering the aquifers and rivers and exporting it in bottles.

What do you drink apart from wine?
There is a local saying that it takes a lot of beer to make good wine. I enjoy beer and I'm one of the people who never buys the same beer twice - I like to try different ones. I like the occasional good vintage scotch or a decent German Schnapps.

What's your party trick?
Drinking more than everyone else! Also, pretending to open beer bottle with my socket - I only have one eye… not as a result of jousting, either! When I was 15 a (now) ex-friend was being foolish and pointed a .22 air rifle at me. It went off point blank and the pellet's still in my skull. I tried wearing a glass eye for a while but it was just a pain. That's why I wear the patch instead.

What's one interesting or unusual fact about you many people wouldn't know?
I've never been to University. I've trained in Germany.

What pets do you have?
Two dogs, a cat and 19,760 Pinot Noir vines!

Who would you most like to share a glass of wine with?
Edward III. It was during his reign that English became the official language instead of French.

mike just

How did you find out about being a direct descendant of King Edward III?
It's something we've always known about in my family, hence why I - and my son - have the middle name Edward. When I was ten, my grandma showed me pictures of these guys, real warrior kings, and my life's goal since then was to visit the castles they built and the places they'd conquered... and one day build a castle on a hill myself. I have one-and-a-half hectares set aside at the top of the vineyard to build a large stone-based house with fortified walls, a tower and underground cellar - I guess that's a castle, isn't it?

So how did that lead to sword fighting and jousting?
It was something I'd always wanted to do, and when I decided to become a winemaker, I was much keener to go to Europe than somewhere closer. While I was there, I got to meet other people with the same interest and discovered there's a big following for medieval battle re-enactments, with lots of huge events at real castles. It became my hobby while I lived in Germany, learning winemaking.

Any good battle stories?
We were at a medieval festival in the Bavarian hills, and one of our group was an enthusiastic clubber. He discovered in the local village that there was nightclub and the owner'd said that if we went down there and had a swordfight, we'd get free drinks all night. We marched down from the hills in full armour expecting it to be a small nightclub, only to discover a few thousand people! The owner started plying us with drinks as soon as we got there and by the time we got to fighting - amidst music, lights, dry ice - we'd all had a lot to drink by that time! Our friend who'd organised it was a bit slow in one move we'd practiced and… well, I split his head open with a broadsword. Blood everywhere, and everyone thought it was fabulous, that it was part of the act. Luckily, he was fine, and wore it as his badge of honour, but we decided such events were probably not the best thing for us, especially if they involved lots of free drinks beforehand!

What would you like to do before you go to the great vineyard in the sky?
To sit under the English oak my wife Paula and I planted at the top of our hill on the last day of last millennium. It'll be the back courtyard of the castle. I'd like to be sitting under that tree looking down at the castle that I built, and the vineyard that I planted, and the family that I brought to the world, drinking vintage Pinot that I made myself with friends, thinking that I did what I planned when I was 10 years old.

wine
Mike's passion and individuality is reflected in the wines he makes. Although he specializes in red varieties, Clayridge Sauvignon Blanc

marks a new direction into the aromatic whites that Marlborough's famous for. Rich yet vibrant, it has intense melon and passionfruit aromas balanced with a hint of citrus, and its complex tropical fruit palate results in a long, fresh finish.

Mike loves Pinot's balance and versatility: "It's a wine that reflects what's been put into it. Great Pinot is a great experience." Clayridge Pinot Gris is a complex, full-bodied wine with ripe pear aromas, toasty wild honey and stone fruit notes and a rich, creamy textured finish.

He's especially proud of the Excalibur Reserve Pinot Noir. Picked from the dry upper slopes of the vineyard, its small concentrated berries make this deep ruby wine a special experience. With rich wild cherry and exotic spice aromas, it's a complex yet approachable wine, with soft smoky oak flavours, ideal for your next medieval banquet, perhaps?

vineyard

Set high on a steep hillside hand-planted by Mike and Paula, Clayridge Vineyards is one of the highest sites in Marlborough, perfect for Pinot. Unlike other vines in the region, these specially selected drought-resistant vines thrive without irrigation or spraying, producing, along with Mike's other environmentally friendly practices, small, intense bunches that create wines of great character and individuality.

Clayridge also has two other boutique vineyards growing exclusively for it: Escaroth Estate on another hillside in Marlborough's Taylor Pass valley, and the Barnhouse Vineyard in the clay-based soils of the Wither Hills.

New neighbours Cloudy Bay and Seresin Estate lend weight to Mike's "gut feeling" about the area's great potential!

Clayridge Vineyards
253 Barracks Road, RD2 Blenheim, Marlborough
ph: [64 3] 572 8151
wines@clayridge.net.nz   www.clayridge.net.nz

hunter's wines

hunter's wines

gary duke - chief winemaker

After bumming round Europe and New Zealand and doing lots of different jobs - "none of which lasted more than four months!" he says, abashedly - Gary Duke ended up working in the big Melbourne breweries. "It was great… and a great education," he says. Ending up in winemaking at the ripe old age of 25, he worked in wineries in Victoria before his fascination with New Zealand compelled him to move to Marlborough and Hunter's Wines in 1991. Since then, his meticulous attention to detail and passion for sparkling and aromatic whites has confirmed his reputation as one of the country's leading winemakers.

Hunter's Wines has its own fascinating story. The combined dream of Jane Hunter and her late husband, the visionary Ernie (who was tragically killed in a car accident at age 37), Hunter's is a fiercely independent, family-owned winery, managed by the driven and renowned Jane, who's been awarded an OBE for service to the wine industry and been described in London's Sunday Times as "the star of New Zealand wine". With a passion for quality, not quantity, Jane and Gary have ensured that Ernie's legacy has lived on in the enviable list of accolades their wines have won, with more than 100 Gold Medals to date.

It's an interesting set up over there… how is it working for a woman in such a male-dominated industry?
We're a small winery, but luckily I get on very well with Jane! I've been here at Hunter's for over 16 years now so I suppose if we were going to have a major blue, we would've had it by now. Interestingly, the top three people here - myself, Peter Macdonald and Jane, are all Aussies, but we've been here for some time now.

What are the differences you've noticed between the Australian and New Zealand wine industries?
The main thing is that we've got good, cool nights, good fruit expression with strong aromatics, though we can't make the Bordeaux reds like Cabernet and Merlot - they look like they've been blended with Sauvignon Blanc. But did I mention we make bloody good Pinot??

How important are prizes?
They are good to get but if you don't get one then big deal. I think there's too many wine shows now, and it means they've lost their importance a bit.

What makes a good winemaker?
Attention to detail and being flexible. You need to make sure everything's right - once it's in the bottle you can't get it back out again.

Art vs science in winemaking - your thoughts?
Well, you have to have a bit of science, but a lot of my decisions are made in the shower in the morning, going by gut feeling!

Corks vs screwtops?
I wish it was corks but I'd have to say screwtops. Corks are nice and I like pulling a cork out, but there's so much variability in the damn things! Corks are essential for sparkling wines, though - I'm a traditionalist that way - popping the cork on a good bottle of fizz really sets the mood or occasion!

Do you have kids?
Yes I have two: my daughter's 25 and my son's 23. They were born in Australia but they follow the All Blacks, the little buggers!

Do they want to be winemakers too?
No - they've grown up around the cellar, helping out when they were growing up. My daughter's done vintages in Australasia and Europe but she only sees it as means to an end - working hard, getting some cash and travelling on. My son appreciates wine but he's not really into winemaking either.

gary duke

Do you consider yourself Australian or Kiwi?
I consider myself Aussie, but in another four years I'll be Kiwi. The boys in the cellar think I should barrack for New Zealand, given that by then I'll've been here for 20 years - though that might make it a bit boring in the smoko room then!

Do you have any other interests apart from winemaking?
I love big game fishing - especially Yellow Fin tuna. I once caught a 45 kilo monster on a 15 kilo line and it took nearly three hours to land! We caught three of the things and got them smoked - we had smoked tuna coming out our ears, especially as you don't need to eat much to enjoy it!

What's your party trick?
Half can't be repeated! Playing harmonica - playing until 2 am and driving everyone nuts (people think I'm tone deaf but I don't!)

What do you do when someone pours you or brings you a bad glass of wine?
If someone was quite proud of it, I used to say "that's okay" and try to be quiet about it. But I got caught out a few times when I did say something like that about a wine that wasn't that good, because people'd say "Well, Gary Duke thought it was alright" and I found it wasn't great for my credibility and reputation. Now, I find I'm better off saying what I really think. I remember once Mick Morris (of the renowned Morris Winery in Rutherglen, Victoria where I used to work) getting out all his Muscats and asking people to try them. He got to one that most people at the tasting should've thought was crap, though most said how nice it was. Only a couple were really honest, and it turned out he'd actually put it in there to see if people would pick it up and say something. In my book, if it's crap, it's crap!

Who would you most like to share a glass of wine with?
Catherine Zeta Jones 'cos I think she's spunky!

Who would you least like to share a glass of wine with?
Michael Douglas, of course!

wine

Reflecting Gary's love of Marlborough's aromatic white wines, Hunter's portfolio boasts outstanding, prize-winning examples, including the Marlborough Sauvignon Blanc, which, like the Gewürztraminer, was sourced entirely from the Wairau Valley.

Hunter's Marlborough Sauvignon Blanc is a classic Marlborough Sauvignon Blanc, with a typically capsicum and gooseberry bouquet, with hints of ripe tropical fruits. A complex, multi layered palate of melon and peach is well balanced by the fruits' natural acidity. It's a great match for light summery food like asparagus, seafood, quiche, goats cheese, pasta with a rich basil sauce, or Thai seafood or stir fry dishes with lots of basil. Great for a picnic or to enjoy alfresco!

Hunter's Gewürztraminer, is an intriguingly aromatic Gewürz (as they call it in the business), redolent of Turkish delight, with spicy ginger aromas. Yum! Appealing and easy to drink - reflected in its Gold Medal and Trophy at the Liquorland Top 100 last year - it's soft and full-bodied, bursting with fresh apricots, ginger and a touch of spice showing through. Great again with lightly spiced curries, stir fried white meats and Thai food.

Sourced from seven specially selected Wairau vineyards and hand-crafted from small, concentrated bunches of fruit, the Gold Medal-winning Marlborough Pinot Noir was the star of the Perth Royal Wine Show. With a medium intensity bouquet showing ripe plums, black cherries and ripe fruits, it's a soft and full-bodied wine with juicy Pinot fruit flavours and a hint of earthy complexity, with a lovely persistence of flavour that Gary reckons is ideal with herb duck breasts and peach salsa or any light game meal.

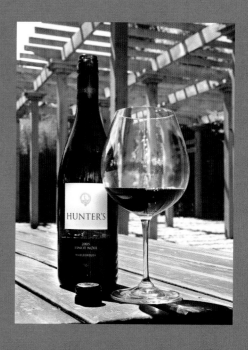

vineyard

Boasting a Marlborough garden full of native trees, shrubs and grasses that reflect the original native flora of the Wairau Valley's dry plain, and with regular sculpture displays in the garden, Hunter's Vineyard is a unique attraction, especially during its annual Garden Marlborough Festival, held in the first weekend in November, which is now recognised as one of New Zealand's most prestigious and popular events of its kind. The Festival features a week of garden tours, workshops with international speakers and a gala fete. For more information, visit the website at www.garden-marlborough.com.

The celebrated artist Clarry Neame is the vineyard's artist in residence. Working in oil, his work is renowned for evoking emotional responses, and includes a diverse range of subjects and styles, including floral oil pointillism, abstracts, landscapes, figurative paintings and portraits with both the brush and palette knife. Selected works are available for sale in the gallery.

Hunter's Wines (NZ) Ltd
Rapaura Road, Blenheim, Marlborough
ph: [64 3] 572 8489   NZ Freephone: 0800 486 837
wine@hunters.co.nz   www.hunters.co.nz
Cellar Door: Open Daily 9.30am - 5pm
Restaurant: Open Daily for Lunch 11.30am - 3pm; and Thu - Sat for Dinner from 6pm during Summer
Open Daily for Lunch 12pm - 2.30pm; and Thu - Sat for Dinner from 6pm during Winter

montana brancott winery

montana brancott winery

patrick materman - regional winemaker

When asked about the best bit of advice he'd ever been given, Montana Brancott's Regional Winemaker Patrick Materman, who also leads the Montana winemaking team, cites his mum telling him to give up a job as a windsurfing instructor at Club Med to take up a trainee winemaker job at Montana's Tamaki Winery in 1990. And what about the worst advice? "My mum telling me to give up a job as a windsurfing instructor at Club Med to take the winemaking job!" he says with a laugh.

Also a yachtsman of some repute, you could say he has saltwater in his veins, but that'd ignore the wine that bubbles through them too. Although he loves his sailing, running his own yacht charter business and sometimes getting rescued by the Coast Guard, winemaking (especially Pinot Noir) is his passion. This is reflected not only in juggling his day job with his own little backyard winery, which he runs from his garage, but in the swag of Gold Medals and awards Montana's wines have won since he became senior winemaker in 1997.

So what are some of the challenges facing you, making such a wide range of wine styles?
I'd have to say the length and complexity of vintage: mine starts late Feb-early March and runs well into May! It's a long vintage and you have to have your head around making such a diverse range of wine styles, which all require very different methods... but I also find that very interesting and challenging.

How many bottles in your cellar?
A fair few hundred, but a lot of those would be those I made at home - we've got a little vineyard and winery in the garage at home so I potter around making wine there - no, the vineyard's not a hydroponic job in the garage! - only the winery's in there (laughs)!

How big's your home vineyard?
It was just a bit of a hobby before and I had about 400 - 500 vines with deer on the rest of the land, but now I've pulled everything out and replanted the whole property with Sauvignon Blanc.

How does working in your home winery inform your work at Brancott (and vice-versa)?
Where does the trial work happen, at home or work (laughs)? There's a few things I try at home like delayed malolactic ferments (when tart malic acid is converted to softer-tasting lactic acid). It usually runs better at warmer temperatures, but the garage is cold over winter! It's nice doing things on a small scale and trying to be creative when you don't have all the equipment to do it.

What do you do to relax?
Sailing's first and foremost, especially on my boat Caravita (which is Italian for "rich life") - but also a bit of diving, cooking, woodwork... and windsurfing, of course!

What's your party trick?
I can carry a whole heap of wine glasses up my arm - a few dozen wineglasses - it's a trick I was taught as a wine waiter in my youth.

How many's a few dozen?
A good three dozen.

How do you carry them up your arm?
You criss-cross them up your arm and then form another stack over the first one - and it's amazing how many you can carry to the table and still have a free hand... it does take a bit of practice!

What do you do when someone pours you or brings you a bad glass of wine?
Probably make use of the spittoon! If I don't like it, life's too short to drink bad wine...

patrick materman

Where's the most interesting/beautiful place you've enjoyed a glass of wine - and what were you drinking?
I do an enormous amount of sailing, and about 18 months ago, I was up in the Reef Islands and took the yacht up there to a place called Ureparapara in Northern Vanuatu. There's this idyllic little setting out on the reef there in the middle of nowhere: palm trees right down to the sea. Drinking Montana Reserve Sauvignon Blanc seemed to just perfectly suit the gorgeous setting, the tropical climate and the freshly caught seafood we were feasting on.

Who's the most interesting person you've shared a glass of wine with?
Oz Clarke, the renowned UK wine critic and writer. He was in New Zealand recently and visited Brancott where we had a relaxed outdoors lunch. He's a brilliant raconteur with a great palate. He was also quite partial to some New Zealand micro-brewed beers he'd discovered. One thing I love about the wine industry is all the colourful characters it attracts.

What's the strangest job you've ever had apart from winemaking?
I was a windsurfing instructor in Auckland during the summer holidays when I was a student and it was a job sponsored by Martini, so I had the whole lot: Martini deck chair and hat and towel and umbrella and best of all, a chilly bin full of Martini!

What would you like to do before you go to the great vineyard in the sky?
Cruising, no doubt about it. I'd especially love to do the whole South Pacific and go up to Canada and Alaska - and then down the Eastern seaboard of the US.

What would your last meal be - and what wine would go with it?
A nice hot sunny day, a barbecue with some freshly caught seafood, shared with friends. And some nice wine for summer drinking - like Deutz Marlborough Cuvée Blanc de Blanc or Montana Estates Brancott Sauvignon Blanc.

wine

One of Marlborough's oldest wineries, Montana's renowned for its premium wines, and Patrick's particularly proud of these. The Terroir Series is a limited release series expressly hand-crafted to showcase the unique influence different terroirs (winespeak for vineyard sites) have on premium varieties grown in the same region. The Festival Block Sauvignon Blanc is no exception. A lovely pale straw wine with red capsicum, citrus and olive aromas, it has concentrated peach and capsicum flavours with great length of flavour and is a fantastic example of Marlborough's signature wine. It's the perfect accompaniment to sautéed chicken breast, perhaps served with tapenade and a fresh garden salad. Fantastic now, it'll gain toasty complexity with careful cellaring.

Sourced from a terraced hillside at the head of the Brancott Valley, the Montana Terraces Pinot Noir is a flagship wine which represents the best of Pinot Noir. Showing complexity and a harmonious balance between fruity richness and silky, supple tannins, it has lifted dark berry and cherry aromas, with hints of spice and chocolate. With a wonderful, warm, dark plum and berry palate, its density's balanced by the fruit's sweet ripeness, and make it a brilliant and elegant match to a wide range of dishes, especially game and mushrooms. Why not try it with a porcini mushroom risotto, or something more exotic like hare, venison... or even grilled ostrich?

Saving only the finest reserve Chardonnay grapes for the Montana Reserve, Patrick's crafted an intensely flavoursome wine in the Marlborough Chardonnay. With an elegant, spicy bouquet showing rich white peach and lemon zest, it's complemented by a creamy, toasty, oaky palate redolent with intense peach and nectarine flavours, balanced by spicy oak, butterscotch and an oatmeal texture. Dry in style, it will develop even more smoothness and complexity with cellaring.

vineyard

As Marlborough's oldest vineyard, Montana's Brancott Winery is a must-see for tourists. You can take a winery tour, with the opportunity to see Brancott's revolutionary new grape tipper tanks, and after tasting some of Montana's premium wines, purchase them from the cellar door, which also includes a wide array of wine paraphernalia.

Brancott's restaurant seats 150 people in an elegant atmosphere enhanced by giant riverstone fireplaces and copper uplighters. It's the ideal place to enjoy world-standard cuisine which perfectly complements Montana's award-winning wines, with an alfresco courtyard dining area open during summer.

Montana Brancott Vineyards
RD4 Riverlands (State Highway One), Blenheim, Marlborough
ph: [64 3] 578 2099
brancottcellardoor@pernod-ricard-nz.com   www.montana.co.nz
Cellar Door : 10.30am - 3pm Daily   Restaurant : 10.30am - 3pm Daily

stoneleigh

stoneleigh

jamie marfell - senior winemaker

Despite being voted Winemaker of the Year by the prestigious Swedish Gourmet magazine and winning Gold and Top 100 at the Sydney International Winemaker Challenge, you won't find a bloke as unassuming and self-deprecating as Jamie Marfell, winemaker at Stoneleigh, one of Marlborough's oldest and most singular vineyards. He's as modest as his tennis shorts aren't!

Growing up on a farm in the region, overlooking the grapevines, winemaking was "inevitable", especially working in the vineyards on his summer holidays. That, and a revelatory "heavy wine drinking experience in my fourth year at uni," he says with a laugh. After completing Lincoln University's prestigious winemaking diploma, he worked around New Zealand before returning to his hometown, Blenheim, with his partner and two young daughters.

Jamie doesn't just work with a minimalist approach to his tennis shorts, but also to Stoneleigh's unique wines, using environmentally sustainable practices that not only enhance the fruits unique characteristics, but ensure that the love he lobs into his award-winning wines goes back into the region as well.

Tell us about sustainable winegrowing.
It's a new movement showing some focus on what we're actually doing, I guess it's a better practice and reflects the move towards greener wines, greener wineries, greener vineyards, greener winemaking practices, which are sustainable as well, It's all about managing your vineyard and winery to look after the environment and people, while still producing the best wine you can do. I guess it's about questioning management decisions with a long term sustainable vision.

How long have you been doing it for?
About the last 4-5 years. I guess it's a movement that's only been going over the last few years. As far as our vineyard practices, I guess we've been questioning our spray usages - I mean Stoneleigh's very unique in that our soils are very low in nutrients and from a vineyard point of view, we've got to be very aware of what we're doing to the environment for the longevity of the vineyard, what we're doing regarding mulching and cover crops and stuff like that, and putting organic matter back on the vineyards.

But if the soil's richer, doesn't that make the wine better?
Yes and no. The soil is only one part of the terroir. Yes, it does an affect over the style of wine, but hey people luv it. It sorta works that way, but you find richer soils produce greater palate weight (winespeak meaning it's richer in the mouth) - so the beauty of stony soils like ours is that the wines tend to be more perfumed and aromatic (and as the winemaker I try to build weight into the palate with some winemaker magic in the winery).

What's the worst wine faux pas you've ever made?
Well, I once called a wine writer pregnant when she wasn't - I think that comes back to haunt me all the time! I've always wondered about her reviews…

Who's the biggest influence on you as a winemaker?
As the first generation coming through Marlborough, I don't know if I've been that influenced by other winemakers, really. I just think of someone like my father, who was a sheep farmer - I remember when they first planted the Brancott vineyard and I'll always remember my old man saying "grapes'll never grow in Marlborough", and he was completely wrong. Those sort of people always really motivate you…

So he was a bit of negative motivator, then?
(laughs) Yeah, you could say that! I remember when I told him I was going to be a

Serve up the love with plenty of deuce

winemaker and he said "and you'll become an alcoholic as well…" But then, if that was the case, what happens when you become a sheep farmer, I wonder?

Art vs science in winemaking - your thoughts?
Well, I work off a messy desk, so I'd like to think of myself as a bit of an artist!

Corks vs screwtops?
Screwtops, definitely. I wouldn't go near a cork now - on my holidays, I bought a Spanish wine with a cork and struggled to find a corkscrew in the house!

What do you do to relax?
I love spending time with the kids - though you'd hardly call it relaxing! I like playing tennis with the boys - it's a great opportunity to see if I still fit into the shorts! I do watch a lot of tennis on TV which sometimes ends up in my game - though only when I miss, I guess! I go for the big shots without much success - and I can't say there's been any great moments in my tennis "career" so far!

Do you have any pets at all?
No, not at all - but you find once you're a dad that having a pet in the house pulls you up from the lowest rank in the house!

What's the most interesting or beautiful place you've enjoyed a glass of wine - and what were you drinking?
I remember being in a restaurant embedded on a cliff in Phuket, called On the Rocks, looking out over the waves crashing in on the rocks below the cliff, watching the sun fall into the sea as we gorged on crayfish as the waves crashed into the rocks, while we drank a wonderful Marlborough Sauvignon Blanc. It was really romantic, really amazing.

What would your last meal be, and what wine would you drink with it?
I love Thai food, so it'd have to be a Thai banquet - with our wonderful Rapaura Series Pinot Gris, of course!

wine

"I love Sauvignon Blanc for the diversity of styles you can find in Marlborough," Jamie says. "It really reflects the place it was grown." And it's true of Stoneleigh Marlborough Sauvignon Blanc, a ripe, full-bodied Marlborough Sauvignon Blanc which exhibits all the lifted citrus and mineral aromas typical of a good Marlborough "savvy" grown in stony Rapaura riverbed soils. With passionfruit and grapefruit aromas and a concentrated, tropical, passionfruity flavour, it's best enjoyed "young and exuberant", either slightly chilled on its own or with delicate white meat and seafood dishes, although it could be cellared carefully over the next couple of years.

"We've been making Pinot Gris for five years, and it's exciting to see how it's performed, especially as it's taken off in Waipura and North Canterbury," Jamie says. "And trying to change your winemaking techniques to make a better wine from different styles and regions - that's a great learning, motivating experience."

And the exclusive Stoneleigh Rapaura Series Marlborough Pinot Gris is a great drinking experience of which he's especially proud. A powerful succulent wine grown only from the most intensely-flavoured selected Pinot Gris grapes grown on the Rapaura Series block, it bursts with ripe pear, peach and sweet melon aromas, with a textured, creamily complex palate of sweet, ripe stone fruit and a touch of spice. Although best enjoyed now, Jamie reckons it'll develop even more luscious, creamy, toasted honey characters over the next two to five years.

"Pinot - it's just one of those varieties where you can make a meal of it if you don't know what you're doing and you get the most satisfaction if you can do it right," Jamie says. Stoneleigh Marlborough Pinot Noir is a most satisfying wine indeed. A soft, supple wine crafted from small, concentrated grapes with the classic cherry, raspberry and dark plum characteristics of a great Marlborough Pinot. A deep ruby red, ripe dark berry and cherry flavours dominate the palate, with lingering fruit sweetness tempered by fine integrated tannins (winespeak for "dryness in red wine"). It's best enjoyed with succulent red meat dishes like lamb, game or veal, drizzled in red berry or mushroom sauces.

vineyard

Set on a now-defunct riverbed on the northern side of the Wairau Valley - called the "Golden Mile" for the profusion of high quality wine it produces, Stoneleigh takes its name from the riverbed's stony soil, which infuses Stoneleigh's wines with their exceptional quality and concentrated, aromatic flavour. How? Because they reflect heat back onto the vines, the stones help to enhance the ripening process, and within the soil create the ideal growing environment.

One of Marlborough's oldest vineyards, Stoneleigh boasts blocks of vines that are up to 20 years old, including Riesling, Sauvignon Blanc, Chardonnay, Merlot, Pinot Noir - and of course, the new Pinot Gris vines Jamie's so excited about.

Stoneleigh Marlborough
Main Road South, Blenheim
ph: [64 9] 5708400   NZ Freecall: 0800 503 000
information@stoneleigh.co.nz   www.stoneleigh.co.nz

koura bay wines

koura bay wines

geoff smith - owner and winegrower

Having been a primary school teacher, a shop-owner, an all-round cricketer and fisherman, Geoff Smith was working in insurance when he and his wife Diane decided they didn't want to grow old in the Smoke. Having enjoyed wine all his life, he decided to get into wine growing - mainly to "get out of the road and out of the kitchen," he says with a laugh. But while being a jack of all trades might make most a master of none, Geoff's wines can now be found in the best restaurants and premium outlets around the world, of the calibre of Gordon Ramsay in London and Glasgow, the Peninsula Hotel in Hong Kong and Antoines in Auckland.

But despite their international reputation, Koura Bay Wines are a family affair: one of the things Geoff loves best is sharing them with family and friends, and with his kids joining him in the business, he has ample opportunity, though there's a "catch": as he puts it, "I only have about a hundred bottles in the cellar - I can't keep the family out of it!"

How did you get into winemaking?
Fell into it by accident, really! My wife and I were living in Auckland, working in middle management in a big insurance company, and getting close to 50, decided we didn't want to grow old in Auckland - I'm from the South Island and missed the space. So, looking for somewhere we'd like to go when we retired, we chose the top of the South Island because it's halfway between her family home and mine. From a five acre block it grew into a 20 acre block because I needed to get myself out of the road in the kitchen. What could we do with it? I had a cricket buddy who was a rural valuer and we got him to look at our block to see what we could do with it, and because he was into grapes - one of the first growers in Montana - we picked a grape block which we planted in 93, and it just grew from there.

What do you love best about what you do?
I think it's people's enjoyment of the finished product - that's always particularly satisfying, and it's also the fact that it's from vine to wine - the total process and you're not part of a process, you've got the overview from start to finish.

How did you get up to speed?
Well, I chose to let the experts make the wine - and I chose to grow it. So effectively I'm the grower and marketer of our product but we do have an employed winemaker - a group of three winemakers Simon Waghorn, Sam Smaill and Paul Gordon, an Australian who's doing the Pinots. We supply some of our fruit to Whitehaven Wines, and that's how we got the connection of having access to their winemaking there.

What's your favourite grape varieties and why - white and red?
Pinot Noir's the red grape I'm most familiar with, and that's the Persian cat of grape varieties - it's the seductive one, the one you strive to perfect: it gets you if you're not careful.

You seemed to have set yourself a particularly tricky challenge starting out planting Pinot!
Yep - particularly as it's planted in quite young riverbed soils, from windblown loess so it's about as different from Burgundy as you can get, you wouldn't get a drop of limestone for 40 miles, yet, the fruit characters are quite Burgundian - so yes, it's quite amazing, and it's something you have to keep working at.

Are you a good fisherman?
I thought I was a reasonable fisherman but they were bringing in quota systems for NZ fishing and I had to decide whether I wanted to be a fisherman or stay doing what I was doing at the time which was primary teaching, and with a mortgage and five kids, I stayed with the government job.

What's the strangest job you've ever had apart from winemaking?
I spent some time as a freshwater eel fisherman; and I also fished for crayfish as well.

What's your favourite hangover cure?
Kino - sea urchin roe… it's deadly! If you can get one of those down you, you're ready to face the rest of the day.

What happens if you don't have sea urchin roe to hand?
(laughs) Well, I guess you have to suffer! Or try the hair of the dog!

Who is your favourite cartoon or superhero?
(groans) I don't know about superheroes, but I love Homer Simpson, because underneath all his crassness and stupidity, he's still a basic human being…

Does that reflect you?
(laughs) I'm not the best person to ask if he reflects me!

What would your last meal be - and what wine would go with it?
A decent Riesling for aperitif, crayfish and champagne, creamed scallops with Chardonnay, a main course of groper tongues and cheeks with Pinot Noir, and sheep and goat's cheese with crackers and a lovely Sauvignon Blanc to finish.

wine
Hand-grown at Koura Bay and made to Geoff's exacting standards, every Koura Bay Wine tells a story - not just of where or how they were grown, but about the Marlborough wine region as well. Crafted by winemaker Sam Smaill, the flagship Awatere Valley Sauvignon Blanc is named after the valley in which the Koura Bay vineyard and homestead are nestled, in the shadows of Mount Tapuaeouenuku, the Kaikoura Ranges' highest peak.

The award-winning Awatere Valley Sauvignon Blanc is a full flavoured, medium bodied wine with a complex bouquet of fresh citrus, grapefruit and white currant with an intriguing mineral undertone, and abundant citrus and grapefruit flavours, with a long and refreshingly crisp finish. Geoff's most proud of this wine, especially since it won the coveted Top 100/Blue Gold at the prestigious Sydney International Wine Show. He reckons it's ideal with Marlborough green-shell mussels, or drinking with tapas or alfresco lunches.

After lunch, while enjoying the cheese platter, you could try the Awatere Valley Pinot Gris (also made by Sam), whose quince, pear and apple flavours and rich, soft texture make it a perfect match with hard cheeses like Parmesan, Gouda and Cheddar. But it's also

great with dishes featuring mushrooms, pork or creamy pasta.

Created by winemaker Paul Gordon, the Blue Duck Pinot Noir is a medium bodied, silky wine with generous dark berry and plum fruit flavours and a lingering and sumptuous finish, which has been awarded Gold Medals in both New Zealand and the US, as well as being named one of New Zealand's Top Ten Pinot Noirs by the prestigious Cuisine Magazine. It's the ideal accompaniment to all game, lamb and roast vegetable dishes, which should keep well if cellared carefully.

vineyard

On the banks of the Marlborough's Awatere River, Geoff and Diane Smith carefully manage Koura Bay Estate, hand-planting and picking Sauvignon Blanc, Pinot Noir, Pinot Gris and Riesling. Described as "the jewel in the crown" of Marlborough, the Awatere Valley's mild climate and breathtaking scenery means wine with concentrated, complex flavours and maximum drinking enjoyment.

Although there's no cellar door as such, you can purchase wines via mail order, or getting in touch with Koura Bay's distributors (details on the website). And if you're in the region, you may taste and purchase wines at the Station Café in nearby Seddon. However, if you'd like to drop by the winery, email or phone Geoff and Diane and let them know you're coming - they'd love to see you!

Koura Bay Wines
Nursery Road, Seddon, Awatere Valley, Marlborough
ph: [64 3] 578 3882
info@kourabaywines.co.nz   www.kourabaywines.co.nz

The Station Café
State Highway One, Seddon, Marlborough
ph: [64 3] 575 7902
www.marlborough-cafe.co.nz

CAMSHORN

WAIPARA

camshorn

camshorn

martin tillard - vineyard manager

Ebullient, gregarious and with a deep mellifluous voice to match, Martin Tillard mightn't be tiny, but he's a barrel of laughs. First discovering wine when he worked in a bottle shop while at university in the early 90s, he was a winemaker for "four or five vintages before I started realising that a wine's quality is so defined and determined by the vineyard that I got out of the factory and into the vineyard", becoming a viticulturalist - or winegrower, as he prefers to call himself "without sounding too hairy fairy, mind!" - in 1996. Having done his first ever vintage with Camshorn's winemaker Mark Hocquard (and worked in that very same bottleshop with Corbans' Tony Robb), Martin works closely with Mark to fully express (winespeak for "bringing out the soil's characteristics") the vineyard's very unique terroir (winespeak for "location, location, location") in its wines, with his unique perspective on all aspects of production from vine to wine imbuing Camshorn's wines with as much character as his own!

Was it hard to move from winemaking to viticulture?
No - I think it's a real bonus because having worked in wineshops and wineries, I think I have more of a feel for what people want in their wines. Winemakers think about what the final style will be like, and a lot of my work is about helping the grapes present the flavour profiles for the wines we're trying to make. I suppose I have a unique perspective, having worked on both sides of the vineyard fence, and having some knowledge of the winemaker's vision for the end product, means that working closely with a winemaker and friend like Mark, we can better achieve that vision. Our close working relationship means that together, we can make Camshorn's wines what they are. Um, does that make us sound too much like boyfriends?

What do you love best about what you do?
The thing I love best is that each year, we can pour out a bottle of wine and share it with friends and say "That's what we did this year" - reminiscing about all the work we had to do, you know, like all the rain that came before harvest that we managed to get through, and pull it off… How cool is that, pulling out a bottle of wine, different to last year's, and saying "That's what we did this year"? It's an amazing sense of achievement.

What time do you get up for work?
Ten minutes before it starts - I'm a shocker! In fact, my wife (a speech therapist) goes to work earlier than me, 30 minutes' away in Christchurch, and if she goes too early and turns the alarm off, she has to ring and get me out of bed. I'm originally a city boy, unlike all the other guys, who are country boys and used to waking up early. I start work at 7.30 am now, but I still struggle with it. I can play all night, but getting up for work… I'm still not used to it!

When's the best time?
Harvest - it's so exciting: you've spent the whole year setting the vineyard up and ready to go, and you're starting to click. For me, it's just a huge time for celebration - everybody's just into getting the fruit and it's just the best time and really enjoying it, you can eat the grapes, they're so tasty and you can see your year's work.

Is there a particular vintage experience you remember?
Probably one of the funniest is from my first vintage - Mark and I had to dig out a press of Pinot skins. I was new to the industry and thought I had to keep up with Mark, who as it turns out, is called Chopper because he comes from a very famous wood-chopping family and used to be the South Island jiggerboard champion, and he's built like the proverbial brick outhouse - he's a big boy, and he didn't have an ounce of fat on him back then - and there was me, just a student, trying to keep up with him. He got all these Pinot skins on his shirt and ripped it off, and here's this bronzed Adonis with a six pack - I realised then that I shouldn't try and keep up with him again… in fact, I needed a cup of tea and a good lie down to recover!

You don't look exactly tiny yourself!
Yes, but I'm built for comfort, not speed!

Who's the most interesting person you've shared a glass of wine with?
For the sake of my marriage, I'd have to say my wife! No, seriously, it's always fun to drink a good bottle with her.

Best wine tosser story?
People like that really bug me because wine is more than just snobbery - it's about enjoyment… Goodness! Well, probably when I was still working in the bottle shop listening to a bloke looking at dessert wines while he tipped them on the side, watching the air bubble go up and down, telling his wife that you could determine the wine's quality by how quickly it moved through the bottle, because of its thickness and concentration.

Can you?
(laughs) Let's just say I had to bite my tongue on that one!

What would you do if you weren't a viticulturist/winegrower?
I'd have to say being retired. I realised early on that being idle was the best pursuit for me!

What's distinctive about your label?
The most distinctive thing is the terroir - we have half on hills, half on the flat, four distinctive soil types, there's a complexity of micro-climates within the site that enable us to make such unusual terroir based wines. The wines are really mapped out according to their soil type, which means that you could plant the same variety on two different soils and it'd taste different. It's cool that we can really express the sites the grapes are growing on - that's the thing I love about it the most.

wine

With its varied mini-climates, Camshorn produces a diverse range of wines. Grown on Domett Clays, a site with high water-holding potential and heavy clay below the loam, Camshorn's Pinot Noir is a deep garnet-coloured wine with aromas of black cherry and plum, with traces of subtle oak vanilla and clove in the bouquet. It's bursting with a generous wild berry and chocolate palate (winespeak for "flavour") with savoury notes of herb and cracked pepper. It's ideal with seared venison cutlets, perhaps accompanied with roasted baby beetroot and mint jus, and will reward careful cellaring for up to six years.

Riesling's one of the best white wines for cellaring, and Camshorn's Classic Riesling is a, well, classic example. Grown on the Glasnevin Gravels, a free-draining part of the vineyard, the Classic Riesling is a rich, spicy wine, with aromas of nectarine, spice and honeysuckle. On the palate, it exhibits spicy peach with overt apple strudel and honey flavours. Martin loves it with char-grilled hoisin pork or other Asian dishes, and says it'll develop a toasty richness and complexity for up to eight years.

Carefully harvested, Camshorn Pinot Gris is a wine Martin's especially proud of. Long, warm, Autumn days and cool nights allowed for extended ripening, resulting in a richly textured Pinot Gris with spicy aromas of pear and cinnamon. Drinking offers pear, mandarin and mineral characters which truly express the site's soils, finishing with lively citrus flavours, making it a perfect match for a galantine of chicken breast, stuffed with pear and lime zest. While drinking well now, it'll reward careful cellaring for two to three years, allowing the spicy characteristics to develop further.

vineyard

With a slightly cooler climate and slightly higher rainfall than the more famous Marlborough, Waipara wines like Camshorn's - particularly the Rieslings - are noted for their intense zingy and scented aromas, resulting in renewed interest in this hitherto neglected region.

Formerly a Suffolk sheep farm, Camshorn is, as Martin points out, blessed by shelter from prevailing winds and an amazingly diverse array of microclimates, which make each wine express the exact spot it was grown in. Spread over 160 hectares, it was planted with 50 hectares of Riesling and Pinot Noir in 2002, with the remaining land planted in 2003 with Riesling, Pinot Noir and some Pinot Gris.

Because it's a small, boutique, working vineyard, Camshorn doesn't yet have cellar door facilities, but you can find its exceptional wines in any excellent restaurant or premium wine retailer.

Camshorn Wines
Waipara, North Canterbury
ph: NZ Freephone 0800 109 922
customerservice@pernod-ricard-nz.com
www.pernod-ricard-nz.com/Pages/vineyards/vwaipara.html

maude winery

maude winery

sarah-kate and dan dineen - owners and winemakers

Although most of us probably spend too much time in the uni bar, usually only leading to hangovers and regrets, for Dan and Sarah-Kate Dineen, it led to winemaking. While Dan was a "failed architecture student who stumbled across the … winery down the road" in his hometown of Adelaide, SK (as everybody calls her) initially followed in her father's footsteps, studying medicine before falling into her vigneron grandfather's footsteps and becoming a winemaker. Meeting at Brokenwood Winery in Australia's Hunter Valley in 1997, they found "love in the lees." Awwww.

But don't let that soppy image fool you: it's not "walks on the beach" and "candle-lit dinners" for this action-packed pair. When most of us with a hangover would rather curl up on the lounge with an aspirin and a trashy video, you'll find the Dineens water-skiing on Lake Wanaka, or carving up Central Otago's spectacular mountainside runs.

Their exuberant energy and lust for life is reflected in their passion for the best possible wines made from the best regions. Having worked in some of Australia's best wineries, including Brokenwood, Tempus Two and Tower Estate, they've returned to SK's parents' vineyard at Mount Maude to shake things up a bit. Well, everything except the champagne, of course!

What's it like working with your parents/in-laws and your spouse?
Dan: You need a bit of diplomacy but it seems to be working at the moment. We've got a thing called the Conch, and if you're holding onto it, you've got the right to speak.
SK: Give me the conch (they laugh)!

Is there any competitiveness between the two labels Maude and Mount Maude (and what are differences)?
Dan: Not really - they're operating in different markets: Maude's mainly export driven and'll end up much bigger; Mount Maude's a relatively small, only 12 acres, and it sells mainly locally.

What do you like least about what you do?
SK: Well, because we're a small winery, we're totally hands-on. Working with Pinot Noir, your hands get stained with grape juice and end up turning black - people think I'm a mechanic, not a winemaker!
Dan: I'm a bit over gumboots nowadays…

How important are prizes?
Dan: Well, as my trophy wife'd say, "they're a lottery," but I know she loves going up to the podium to collect her prize!
SK: Um, yes, that's true!

What's it like being an Aussie in a Kiwi vineyard?
Dan: You get lots of stick -
SK: Hey! I got lots when I was in Australia!

Do you have any other interests apart from winemaking?
SK: We're both keen snow and water-skiers… oh and golf.
Dan: And we're both into cooking too.

Any good skiing stories?
Dan: When we were in Australia, a group of winemakers who were also keen skiers'd go to Thredbo for the Hunter Valley winemakers' annual ski trip and magnum lunch, which would be held at Kirrela Hut, a restaurant perched on Australia's steepest slope. Every couple'd present and pour a magnum with the label hidden, then ask a series of questions to determine its variety, origin or vintage…

sarah-kate and dan dineen

SK: And it wasn't unusual to demolish 16 magnums and a double magnum of Champers!

Dan: Most of us would try to ski down after lunch -

SK: Well, the stupid ones!

Dan: (laughs) Yeah, there'd be accidents, tree-hugging, backward skiing - all sorts of disarray to annoy the ski patrols!

SK: And the best part was it'd always finish with a snow fight at the bottom, with everybody overjoyed they'd made it -

Dan: But it always ended up out of hand…

SK: I know - I ended up with broken ribs as a result of the snowball fight, not the ski run!

What's the worst disaster at vintage?

Dan: I once had a shocker! There was a big 20-tonne vinamatic at Mount Pleasant - it's a big red fermenter which resembles a cement mixer. Anyway I turned it on with the door open. Ten tonnes of Shiraz flooded down the driveway straight into my boss's office. He wasn't a happy man - he didn't talk to me for a week!

Do you have nicknames in the vineyard?

Dan: We call SK "Crash" 'cos she's tough on the equipment -

SK: Speak for yourself (see story above)!

What's distinctive about your label?

SK: Well, the logo itself is the first label to be actually fire-branded into the label

Dan: Both our previous wineries (Tower Estate and Tempus Two) worked with the philosophy of taking varietals from the region they performed best. We've carried on this philosophy at Maude, choosing three varieties people love drinking right now from three regions considered "hot to trot" at the moment: the right wines at the right time…

wine

Maude's Sauvignon Blanc is youthful but classically Marlborough. Like SK, perhaps? With lively, herbal, grassy aromas and hints of gooseberries, this full-bodied fruit-driven wine bursts with freshness and ripe, zesty gooseberry and lemon-lime citrus characters, balanced by a natural, underlying mineral element. "We bottled it early to capture its exuberant essence," says SK, who reckons all it needs to accompany it are some freshly shucked oysters with just a squeeze of lemon juice.

"Yes, we love Pinot - not just because we're winemakers who like a challenge, but because when you get it right, it's the most

amazing wine," says Dan. Maude Pinot Noir is pretty amazing: a vibrant red-purple wine with luscious plum, dark berry, fruit and spice aromas with ripe cherry plum characters and a velvety texture. Great on its own, but wonderful with twice cooked duck, just the way Dan likes it!

Hand-harvested and crafted, the typically bone-dry Maude Pinot Gris exudes green pears, rosebud, straw and spice aromas, with long honeysuckle, pear and citrus flavours balanced by a complex appley acidity. SK reckons it'll age beautifully, developing even further warmth, richness and complexity over the next seven years, but it's a pleasure to drink now, especially enjoyed over tapas or a mezze plate with friends - though don't ask these two what should go on it! SK likes marinated Kalamatta olives, fried haloumi and hummus, and Dan goes for fine shaved prosciutto or Parma ham. Yum!

vineyard

Set on dramatically steep north-facing slopes with breathtaking views of the beautiful Maungawera Valley, it's easy to see why SK wanted to come home to Mount Maude Vineyard, where she and Dan live and work with SK's parents, the lovely Terry and Dawn. With its free draining soils and basking in Central Otago's famously long autumns, it's the perfect place to grow the Pinot Noir grapes that make Maude's fantastic wines, which like the homestead and tasting room (built from mud-bricks dug and made from Mount Maude earth) are hand-crafted on this spectacular site.

It's one of those places you'll call home as well! Just call or email first, to make sure the welcome mat's out.

Maude Winery
Mount Maude Vineyard, Maungawera Valley, Wanaka, Central Otago
ph: [64 3] 443 8398
Dan: [64 21] 421 990   Sarah-Kate: [64 21] 363 123
info@maudewines.com   www.maudewines.com
Cellar Door: Open by appointment only

chard farm

chard farm

rob hay - owner and winemaker

Despite being a bit of a "lost soul" after university, Rob Hay took off to Germany to study winemaking. "I was always intrigued by the wine industry: I liked the mix of the outdoors and indoors." But there weren't many tertiary opportunities for winemaking in New Zealand in the early 80s, so Rob went where the work - and expertise were. "But I actually met my wife Gerda (who was born in Germany) here!" he says with a laugh. They married around the same time he started the Chard Farm in 1987, and now have three kids.

In addition to his many responsibilities around the Farm and his busy viticultural consultancy, Rob is an avid mountain and motocross biker, enjoying the spectacular scenery of Central Otago atop his bikes - and occasionally from his derby racer!

What do you love best about what you do?
Taking something from the absolute raw product to the final product and being involved in that process all the way through.

What's the worst disaster at vintage?
I once worked at a winery where a press door wasn't closed properly. We were pressing red grapes at the time and the press rotated, the door opened at the bottom, and consequently all wine and skins flowed out of the press within a few seconds and onto the floor of the winery. Everyone stood around in shock, cussing and swearing. We realised the skins had blocked the outlet and the drain so we set up a pump and ended up pumping the skins and wine into a container and managed to rescue about 95% of the wine which actually turned out to be okay despite its time on the concrete winery floor! We labelled it "Milburn Reserve", after the local cement company.

When's the best time?
Vintage is always the buzz time - fruit coming in and everything on a roll. Everybody seems to spark up a few notches. Our house is very close to the winery and we'll invite the cellar crew across for a special meal where we'll drink some good wine - I'll get in a special Burgundy or something. Gerda's cooking skills are legendary in the Valley!

Best bit of advice you've been given in your career?
Way back in 1982, when I first got into the industry, Randy Weaver (the former winemaker at Coopers Creek) advised me that the best thing you can do is taste, buy and try as much wine as you possibly can - and I've tried to do that, believe me!

Worst bit of advice you've been given in your career?
Not to plant grapes in Central Otago. I remember soon after we purchased the Chard Farm in 1987 I happened to overhear someone in the pub say that Chard Farm as a vineyard was "a waste of bloody good Merino country".

What do you do to relax?
Trolley racing isn't relaxing as it's too serious and competitive but I enjoy going "bike bush" in the Central Otago high country. I love mountain biking and off-road motor biking. I used to do it competitively, but my body's no longer as rubbery as it used to be!

What sort of bike do you ride?
A Suzuki DRZ 400 off-roader - the result of a mid life crisis. It's a beauty!

Do you have any other interests apart from winemaking?
Gerda and I do a lot of mountain biking in the area, competing in races around the South Island and also hope to get over to Europe for the Adidas TransAlp challenge one year or maybe the South African Cape Absa Classic - both are mega races!

What music do you listen to at work?
Music's not really allowed here during vintage as I find it a bit too distracting…

What's your party trick?
Well, it used to be removing corks from bottles without a cork screw…

How do you do that?
You whack the base of the bottle with a shoe… it worked about fifty percent of the time. But it's a bit tricky now we're using screw caps. Actually, it's impossible!

Are your kids interested in the wine industry?
The boys especially are starting to develop a bit of an interest as they start getting their heads around what's involved.

Would you encourage them into the wine industry?
That's tricky - you can't expect them to follow along and take over the business, but it'd be a lovely thing if it did happen. I wouldn't push them, though. There are some really lovely examples of families in the wine industry who have done just that, like the Babich family, whom I used to work for; the Seifrieds; or the Nooyens at Vilagrad. Though perhaps my kids could start with something to fall back on - like becoming trolley mechanics?

What's the strangest job you've ever had apart from winemaking?
Working on opening night for a highly disorganised Italian restaurant in Germany where I even had the pizza shovel thrown at me at one stage!

What's one of the hardest things about being a winemaker?
Dealing with wine pretension and wine tossers.

What's distinctive about your label?
The winery itself has been described as "a dramatically aspected vineyard" - it hangs on top of a cliff with a massive hundred metres down to the raging Kawarau River below. It's totally picturesque and spiritual. It's visible from the road and if you've seen the vineyard, you'd understand what it means to "drink the place" - you really get a sense of "drinking our vineyard." It's pretty emotive.

wine

Chard Farm Pinot Gris is a superb wine with a heady perfume of pears, apricots, guava and wild honey. It's a superb wine with opulent, sweet fruit flavours and succulently oily mouth feel, oozing concentrated fruit. Perfect with a light lunch of snapper and a lime and coriander dressing - or just sipping and enjoying!

Finla Mor Pinot Noir is the result of an excellent vintage which has produced "some of the best, most balanced wines we've ever seen" according to Rob. Named after an ancient Celtic warrior ancestor of Rob's, it bursts with fragrant aromas of red berries and plum with subtle liquorice and dark spice notes. With complex weight and texture, its soft velvety tannins integrate beautifully with the swirl of intense flavours. A perfect match for venison with mustard-soy jus and blueberries.

The Tiger Pinot Noir is a single vineyard bottling from grapes grown in the Chard Farm's Tiger vineyard, of which only 200 cases are produced every year! Wines from the Tiger typically display spicy aromatic and broadly structured berries and violets with finely textured layers of tannin. Dark ruby red, with exotic red berry aromas underpinned by mildly spicy and earthy tones, this silky wine is a brilliant match for casseroled wild rabbit - "preferably the high-altitude, oxygen-depleted Central Otago variety!" Rob advises.

vineyard

Chard Farm, Chardonnay - that's what you're thinking, right? Except you'd be wrong. The Chard Farm Vineyard takes its name from the first owner, a Richard Chard of Dorset in England, who came out to New Zealand in the 1860s, lured by the famous Dunstan Gold Rush. He was only 14. After several years of backbreaking work around Dunstan and Gibbston, he finally settled on the old Queenstown coach road on a small one acre block with a few cows and chickens. It stayed in the family until the late 70s, briefly becoming a stonefruit orchard before Rob and his family took it over.

Since then, it's been onwards and upwards. Well, a lot of upwards, given the spectacular and precipitous bluffs that surround the Vineyard. Constructed in 1993, the winery building includes a specialist Pinot Noir cuverie which uses Old World techniques of standing the barrels in bare earth pits to prevent evaporation - or what winemakers call "the angels' share" - by keeping the cellar humid and cool, something especially important in the dry heights of Central Otago.

You'll find the tasting rooms and cellars at the end of a spectacular driveway just a hundred metres past the AJ Hackett Kawarau Bungy Bridge, on the Queenstown outskirts on the way to Wanaka. You may wish to have a drink after your bungy jump - though perhaps not vice versa? Or versa vice?

The Chard Farm Winery
RD 1, Queenstown
ph: [64 3] 442 6110   NZ Freephone: 0800 THE FARM
info@chardfarm.co.nz   www.chardfarm.co.nz
Cellar Door : Open 10am - 5pm Weekdays and 11am - 5pm Weekends

quartz reef

quartz reef

rudi bauer - winemaker

Born in Salzburg, the home of Mozart (though he assures us he has no musical talent) Rudi Bauer arrived in New Zealand in 1985 after completing Degrees in viticulture and winemaking Gumpoldskirchen in Austria and Bad Kreuznach in Germany. He worked at a number of different New Zealand wineries, before meeting his effervescent French business partner Clotilde Chauvet in 1992, and going on to found Quartz Reef with her in 1996 with John and Heather Perriam from Bendigo Station and Trevor Scott, a Dunedin businessman who joined the company two years later.

Clotilde's family has been making Champagne since 1529, and her long heritage - and love of partying - is reflected in Quartz Reef's Methode Traditionelle sparkling wines.

Rudi mightn't share Clotilde's long winemaking pedigree but his passion and meticulousness have won him the coveted Champion Winemaker of 1999 at the Royal New Zealand Easter Wine Show. Literate, thoughtful, artistic - if not necessarily musical! - his approach to winemaking is philosophical and understated - he's certainly not one to "blow his own trumpet". Well, not within hearing, anyway!

How did you and Clotilde meet?
When I was making wine at Rippon Vineyards on Lake Wanaka from '89 to '92, she took over my position as the winemaker.

How did you become friends as a result of that?
Clotilde's French (laughs)! She's a very lively person and she knows how to party!

What made you move to New Zealand in the first place?
After completing my studies at Bad Kreuznach, I thought it was time for me to work overseas. I didn't get a permit for the US or Australia and didn't want to go to South Africa at the time because of apartheid. So I visited Dr Professor Helmut Becker from the Geisenheim Institute and told me to go see the NZ Ambassador in Cologne, who then kindly gave me a lot of winery contacts. I wrote to all of them and Mission Estate expressed interest.

I got a six month work permit for New Zealand and it was easy to get it extended. And because of the seasonal differences, it was also much easier to do vintages in the States as well. Then I met my future wife… and the rest is history.

Who's the biggest influence on you as a winemaker?
Herman Hesse (laughs) - he wasn't a winemaker but he was a great writer. At the end of the day, winemaking comes down to philosophy and he always pointed out that as a person, you shouldn't be afraid of confronting your own desires and fears of your own demise, because it's just a human life, and in his work there's always a sense of that split personality in every human being, and that same inner conflict between those two impulses, sometimes the wolf wins and sometimes you do.

Um, what's that mean for us less philosophical drinkers?
(laughs) Well, I suppose what I mean is that wine - philosophical wine like Pinot - is a "Medium for Communication": it allows you to drift closer to your dreams…

I suppose in relation to Herman Hesse, it means always searching for the boundaries of what Pinot can do and its expression of the site it comes from and the hands who made it - who's the wolf? Is it me? Or the wine?

Wow. Deep, man…
Thanks, grasshopper!

Best bit of advice you've been given in your career?
Think. And always ask why.

Art vs science in winemaking - your thoughts?
I like to see wine as a picture - for example, if you see some of Picasso's work, you don't know why it hits you but it hits you... it's the same with music, if you listen to say, Beethoven's Fifth Symphony or Tom Waits' stuff - they're serious handfuls and very extreme, but they reflect who those people are, with all the pain involved... I'd like to make wines just as complex and thought-provoking: I think if wine can give you the same sensation, that it can lift you somewhere, then I think that'll be a good wine.

How do people react when you tell them you're a winemaker at dinner?
Well, actually I tell people I'm a hairdresser from Gore, a small town in the South Island - they usually don't know what hits them and if they don't get it, I usually keep stringing them along.

What would you like to do before you go to the great vineyard in the sky?
I'd love to play the trumpet, though with my lack of musical talent, I think that'd be a bit tricky. But I love the sound and I suppose I could just go up into the mountains to play it...

wine
Rudi and Clotilde both bring old world experience and new world innovation to their wine portfolio, as well as their own unique perspectives to their different styles.

Quartz Reef's Chauvet Methode Traditionelle is named after the Champagne House Marc Chauvet (Rilly La Montagne), where Clotilde's family have made Champagne for over five hundred years. Made with the same techniques, the Chauvet Methode Traditionelle Vintage 2002 is made from specially selected Central Otago Pinot Noir and Chardonnay grapes, and fermented and aged in the bottle for a minimum of 46 months. With a yeasty, ripe apple and biscuit bouquet, it has a focused and elegant length and persistent mousse awakening ("mousse" isn't chocolate! It's wine speak for the fine, foamy bubbles that make champagne bubbly) and was made to enjoy with fresh oysters and someone desirable...

While Clotilde's expertise is in Methode Traditionelle Champagnoise, Rudi's passion is for Pinot. Quartz Reef's hand-picked Pinot Noir is a bright red wine whose vibrant, softly spicy bouquet bursts with black plum and cherry notes. Well structured with lush, intense fruit flavours, it's balanced by ripe, chalky tannins. Rudi reckons it's a great match for pheasant, rabbit or fleshy fish like tuna,

and has cellaring potential for between five and eight years, where it will gain even further silkiness and depth.

Quartz Reef's Pinot Gris was also hand-picked, reflecting Rudi's meticulous and knowledgeable approach to a variety of styles. A pale yellow wine with rose petals on the nose (winespeak for "bouquet" or "aroma") it's a weighty and lush wine with appealing mouth feel, textural and a lingering finish that makes it ideal with any kind of South Pacific cuisine or seafood, especially fragrant shellfish like crab.

vineyard

Central Otago is New Zealand's youngest and most dynamic wine region, and Bendigo, where Quartz Reef's vineyard is located, is the most exciting new area in Central Otago. "When I first saw the land in 1991," says Rudi, "I was incredibly excited." And that enthusiasm led to Quartz Reef being the first vineyard planted in the area.

So why isn't it called, say, Bendigo Estate or something like that, then? Why Quartz Reef? Well, around 1862, New Zealand's largest quartz reef deposit was found underneath Bendigo's stony soils, and though the "quartz rush" is long over, the winery that bears its name is still producing gems of wine from Bendigo's sun drenched slopes. And a bit of gold too - since its first release in 1998, Quartz Reef has already gained international recognition and acclaim, with Rudi winning Champion Winemaker of the Year at the Royal New Zealand Wine Show in 1999.

Despite all that acclaim, "we're still a small, 'no frills', working winery" Rudi says. The cellar door mightn't be the most glamorous, being in the middle of the Lake Dunstan Industrial Estate, but with wine as good as this, who cares?

Quartz Reef Winery
P O Box 63, Cromwell
ph: [64 3] 445 3084
info@quartzreef.co.nz
www.quartzreef.co.nz

"No Frills" Winery and Cellar Door
Building 10, Hughes Crescent, Lake Dunstan Estate, McNulty Road, Cromwell
(just off SH6 on the Cromwell - Queenstown Road)
Cellar Door : Open Monday - Friday 10am - 3pm or by appointment
Open in summer on some weekends 12pm - 4pm

rabbit ranch

rabbit ranch

john wallace - winemaker

Swapping the pistes to get people - well, pissed! - wasn't much of a stretch for John Wallace. Growing up in Taumarunui on the North Island, only half an hour from the ski fields, he could ski before he could walk. Or something like that. A break from university to be a ski instructor lasted "a few years too many", he says with a laugh. Any good skiing stories? "Sure - plenty! But they're pretty clichéd - the usual yarns about partying in nightclubs with your ski boots still on, sleeping in a different bed every night, the Jacuzzis, the parties, the horror runs, all that… ah, the memories… Hey! This is meant to be a book about wine, not skiing!"

Right. Where were we? Oh, yes. "With global warming in mind", John started studying winemaking as an alternative career. Starting at nearby Chard Farm vineyard in 1997, he moved into the cellar and the winemaking side under the tutelage of Rob Hay, owner and winemaker at Chard Farm. After doing several vintages in California and Oregon - you suspect close to ski fields! - he started working at the Rabbit Ranch in 2003, and it's all gone "downhill" from there…

How did you make the move from skiing to winemaking?
Drinking lots of wine! Oh, and a farming background helps…

What are the similarities / differences between them?
Probably more differences, I'd say. When you're skiing, you try and go as fast as you can, and when you're making wine, you have to take a lot more time. So I suppose winemaking suits you better in your later years… and it's easier on your knees!

What do you love best about what you do?
Getting to chase rabbits round the vineyard on the motorbike. We've got big ones - they like chewing on the young grapevines, unfortunately…

Is there much competitiveness between winemakers in your region?
No, not really. Part of the Ranch's philanthropic programme is to sponsor "unserious" racing - mainly trolley derbies and mountain bike racing. My trolley's a carrot, of course. So while there isn't that much competitiveness as far as wine's concerned, we do take the racing pretty seriously!

Do you have nicknames in the vineyard?
No. But plenty of rabbits!

What makes a good winemaker?
Patience and observance.

Who's the biggest influence on you as a winemaker?
Old Man MacGregor (the former owner of the Ranch) - the things he did in that tractor shed were honestly phenomenal. As the Ranch's founding father, he was truly inspirational and hugely influential.

Best bit of advice you've been given in your career?
"Look out! That tank's about to overflow!"

Worst bit of advice you've been given in your career?
"Too late."

What's your favourite drinking game?
It's called "give me the keys to your cellar and I'll choose a bottle".

What's your favourite hangover cure?
Well, you can only really do it in winter, unfortunately. Go to the top of your favourite ski run, take off your hat and goggles and ski down as fast as you can with your mouth wide open. Lots of cold oxygen's the key.

What about in summer?
Suffer! Or "hare" of the dog…

What do you drink apart from wine?
Beer - and lots of it. Especially micro-brewed pilseners.

How many bottles in your cellar?
Not many because I have too many people coming round to play my favourite drinking game!

What's your favourite movie?
King Kong because it was such an entertaining extravaganza of everything a movie should have in it: drama, irony, love interest, car chases, dinosaur chases.

Who's your favourite cartoon or superhero?
Bugs Bunny 'cos he's funny and Roger Rabbit 'cos he's married to Jessica!

Which five people would you have to your dream dinner party?
George Bush to propose a toast - I'd like to hear that!; Dick Cheney for his thoughts on hunting (though I wouldn't want to be around him with a loaded gun); Britney Spears for a sing-along; Gordon Ramsay to boil the bunny; Kim Jong Il because he looks like such an interesting character; and Borat for entertainment.

What would your last meal be - and what wine would go with it?
Probably a hamburger and chips and two of the great vintages of Domain de la Romanee-Conti Richebourg - magnums, of course. And the burger would have no pineapple or beetroot, of course!

What music do you listen to at work?
It depends on who's working in the cellar at the time - usually rock or something like that that'll keep you moving.

What's distinctive about your label?
Well, the actual label has a big startled rabbit sitting on it with its ears pointing straight up. Contrary to popular belief, it's not a hare - and I should know! As for the wine? Well, it's a great wine for celebrating. It doesn't require a lot of thought - it's a soft, bouncy, cuddly wine with no pretension and lots of flavour!

wine

Although rabbits once overran the Ranch, it's now blooming with grapevines. John has a fine nose for aromatic wine, and these wines are the pick of the bunch. The Rabbit Ranch Sauvignon Blanc leaps into your senses "like the startled rabbit it is," according to John. Bounding with fresh fruit aromas of passionfruit and grapefruit, it also has veggie garden undertones of capsicum, tomato and green beans, which makes it ideal for fresh rock oysters - "or even mountain oysters!" says John - au natural, of course, and with a squeeze of lemon, naturally.

The Rabbit Ranch Pinot Gris jumps out of the glass with fresh, earthy aromas of apples, pears and honeysuckle. And it goes wonderfully with - what did you expect? - rabbit confit! But you could also try it with a wild mushroom risotto on a bed of dandelion leaves.

The Rabbit Ranch is "powered by Pinot", according to John, and its Central Otago Pinot Noir is certainly a powerful drop. "It's a bright-eyed red with hints of the briar patch - and a whiff of gunsmoke!" says John. and fruity with a soft, fluffy tail - sorry, finish - it's ideal for rabbit stews or pies, or any succulent, gamey red meat dish, like rabbit and wild thyme pie, rabbit and wild boar bacon stew, or John's favourite, Angry Pheasant sausages…

vineyard

The Rabbit Ranch is a collaborative venture, formed by a group of vineyards subdivided out of a Central Otago sheep station. This station was once owned by the indomitable and inimitable Mr Mack McGregor, the infamous veggie grower and rabbit nemesis who also ran some sheep on the station. He ended up planting Pinot in the cabbage patch after it was decimated by rabbits one year, and produced the Rabbit Ranch's first vintage out of the old tractor shed - the first wines were fined with Easter eggs and filtered through the old lady's stockings.

Now the station's been split up, the new vineyard owners banded together to form the Rabbit Ranch with the nearby Chard Farm as production partner and John Wallace - who also works at Chard Farm - as winemaker. The Rabbit Ranch's vineyards are all in the Cromwell Basin, predominantly in Lowburn. Thriving on light stony soils which are great for wine - and rabbits!

The Rabbit Ranch
RD 1, Queenstown, Central Otago
ph: [64 3] 442 6110   NZ Freephone: 0800 843 327
warren@rabbitranch.co.nz

popular wine varieties

white wine

Chardonnay
Fruit laden character with a range of flavours varying from apples and citrus through to lush peaches and apricots. Found in almost all regions - Chardonnay is one of the most widely planted grape variety in New Zealand.

Chenin Blanc
Full bodied and fresh, it has honeyed flavours with a crisp finish of peachy and pineapple. Chenin Blanc is native to the region of the Loire Valley, France. A versatile grape, it has prospered in its adoptive countries, including 500 acres in New Zealand.

Gewürztraminer
Known for its crisp and spicy attributes, it is an easily identified varietal. Quite aromatic, it has a floral flavour with characteristics of cloves and nutmeg. It is generally accepted that Gewürztraminer has its origins in the Alsace region of France. You'll find sunny Nelson and Hawke's Bay produce this variety very well?

Pinot Gris
Varying from deep and rich to tangy and light, with citrus flavours and a light floral fragrance. Pinot Gris has origins in Bordeaux, France. Though planted in New Zealand throughout the last century the variety did not gain popularity until the 1990's.

Riesling
A light and delicate wine that ranges from bone-dry to honey-sweet. German in origin, Riesling now has a home in New Zealand's Marlborough region where over half of the New Zealand's plantings exist. Gaining popularity, plantings have doubled in the last decade

Sauvignon Blanc
This explosively flavoured varietal can have a grassy, grapefruity or gooseberry nature. Established as New Zealand's flagship wine in the 1990's, Sauvignon Blanc meets international acclaim and is New Zealand's second most widely planted varietal

Viognier
A rich and complex aroma of apricots and orange-blossoms with a distinctively sweet flavour and subtle acidity.

red wine

Syrah (Shiraz)
Robust, with rich aromas ranging from violets to berries, chocolate and espresso. Originally from the Rhone, it has grown in New Zealand for more than 100 years and performs best in the warmer regions.

Pinotage
Flavours ranging from fruity to peppery and slightly gamy. A cross between Pinot Noir and Cinsaut, or Hermitage, Pinotage was created in South Africa in 1924 and is now planted on 94 hectares in New Zealand.

Pinot Noir
Perfumed, richly flavoured and supple bodied with a velvety texture. Intense aroma of black cherries accented by a spiciness of cinnamon or mint. Famously from Burgundy, Pinot Noir first appeared in the Auckland region during the mid 1970's and is now produced all over New Zealand, flourishing in the cool climate.

Merlot / Blends
Supple and rich, with plummy and berry favours. Merlot is medium-bodied and versatile making it a popular blend with Cabernet Sauvignon. Originating in Bordeaux, Merlot was a relatively latecomer to New Zealand, arriving in the late 1980's. It has made a tremendous impact in a short time, with the number of plantings now competing with Cabernet Sauvignon.

Cabernet Sauvignon
Black currant aroma with nuances of cedar spice and violets. A rich and sturdy wine admired for its complexity. Originating in the Bordeaux region of France, Cabernet was brought to New Zealand from California in 1976. Cabernet Sauvignon are the most widely planted red grape varieties in Auckland, Northland, Waikato and Hawkes Bay.

hayden wood, aka 'woody' – publisher

Not one to shy away from unusual projects, Woody has published a library of beverage books that go beyond the traditional boundaries of their genre. Good Wine, Bad Language, Great Vineyards was another opportunity to turn tradition on its head and show winemakers as they've never been seen before.

Blown away by the huge response after the launch of the Australian edition of Good Wine, Bad Language, Great Vineyards, Woody began to think more about the potential scope of the project.

"My instincts directed me to my homeland New Zealand. We have good wine (some say it's great) and without overstating the popularity of the wines featured in this book, many of these talented winemakers put it on the world stage for more reasons than just Pinot and Sav Blanc."

Woody has a love for all things consumable and this passion spills over to include the personalities he met while creating this book. "It was such an honour to meet the characters standing behind the reputation of Kiwi plonk. I dig you all, you're so bloody good at what you do. You don't need medals; you don't need the awards or the accolades, letters after your names or pronounced quaffy accents to prove your excellence. You're Kiwi's god damn it and the world salutes you. I had a blast and I hope you all continue to blow us away for many years to come."

sunil badami - writer

Sunil Badami likes a drink. Or three. "Let's face it," he says. "Writers can't just be good spellers, they've got to be borderline alcoholics too."

Although he's written for publications in Australia and the United Kingdom - as well as editing the first two Liquid Kitchen books - writing Good Wine, Bad Language, Great Vineyards: Wine Characters of New Zealand proved a particular challenge for Sunil, who returned to Australia from the United Kingdom just two weeks before the project commenced in preparation for the birth of his first child.

As well as asking the book's characters about their lives and work, he also asked for some parenting advice. "Most of the women told me to sleep as much as I could before the baby came, and all the men told me to drink as much as I could." Well, they would, wouldn't they? They're winemakers, after all!

However, with daughter Leela due in the middle of writing, he had to curtail his boozing, just in case his lovely, long-suffering wife April went into labour. "Given how much she had to give up during the pregnancy, I was happy to forego hangovers."

Which he'll be doing for a few good years yet, no doubt.

esmeralda wood - photographer/designer/art director

An accomplished painter and graphic designer, Esmeralda's photographic gift is capturing the personalities of everyday people and making them look like superstars. This, her fourteenth book of photography and design, showcases her creative skills in a fun and vibrant portrayal of an industry steeped in serious tradition.

"It was such a great opportunity to be able to experience the wine industry in New Zealand. Moving around from the North to the South Islands was awe inspring. What a beautiful country. I remember driving through the most beautiful terraine and just being gobsmacked how amazing it looked. When I saw a sign that said - Scenic Route 200m ahead - I burst out laughing.

There were some magical moments whilst working on this project. One that comes to mind is doing the photoshoot of Dan and Sarah-Kate Dineen from Maude Winery. They had organised a helicopter ride for their shoot and to top it off it happened to be the last photos for the book. Wow, what a finale.

Thanks everyone for your beautiful hospitality."